Johann Sebastian Bach

Overtures Nos. 1–2
BWV 1066–1067

Edited by / Herausgegeben von
Harry Newstone

Urtext

EULENBURG

EAS 113
ISBN 3-7957-6513-7
ISMN M-2002-2335-4

Ernst Eulenburg Ltd
48 Great Marlborough Street
London W1F 7BB

Contents / Inhalt

Preface   VI

Vorwort   XI

Overture No. 1 in C major BWV 1066

I.   Ouverture   1   Track 1

II.   Courante   14   Track 2

III.   Gavotte 1 alternativement – Gavotte 2   16   Track 3

Gavotte I d.c.

IV.   Forlane   18   Track 4

V.   Menuet 1 alternativement – Menuet 2   19   Track 5

VI.   Bourrée 1 alternativement – Bourrée 2   21   Track 6

VII.   Passepied 1 alternativement – Passepied 2   23   Track 7

Overture No. 2 in B minor BWV 1067

I.   Ouverture   25   Track 8

II.   Rondeaux   38   Track 9

III.   Sarabande   41   Track 10

IV.   Bourrée I alternativement – Bourrée II   43   Track 11

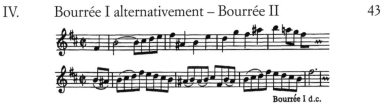

Bourrée I d.c.

V.   Polonoise – Double   45   Track 12

Polonaise d.c.

VI.   Menuet   47   Track 13

VII.   Battinerie   48   Track 14

Preface

From early in the 17th century until the form engaged the interest of Johann Sebastian Bach, various composers had contributed to the development of the orchestral suite, notably and one of the first, Johann Rosenmüller (c.1619–1684), a predecessor of Bach's at the Thomasschule in Leipzig where he was appointed assistant master in 1642 and where, three years later, he published his first work – a collection of instrumental dances entitled 'Paduanen, Alemanden, Couranten, Balletten, Sarabanden mit 3 Stimmen und ihren Basso pro Organo'.

Other German composers, among them Johann Caspar Ferdinand Fischer (c.1665–1746) whose Op. 1 of 8 Overture-Suites 'Journal de printemps' was published in 1695, and later Georg Philipp Telemann (1681–1767) and Johann Friedrich Fasch (1688–1758) also produced instrumental suites of dances. Fasch, who was to become a scholar at the Thomasschule under Bach's immediate predecessor, Johann Kuhnau (1660–1722), wrote a number of orchestral suites in emulation of his admired Telemann and behind so many of his German contemporaries can be discerned the masterful presence of Jean-Baptiste Lully (1632–1687), not least in the innovation of preceding his dances with an imposing 'Ouverture' from which the form eventually took its name. Fasch, later to go into the service of Count Morzin of Lukavec, Bohemia, (who was in 1759 to give Joseph Haydn his first Music-Directorship) was much admired by Bach who hand-copied a number of Fasch's orchestral suites.

From Bach himself, only four such suites have come down to us although Heinrich Besseler who, with Hans Grüss, edited these works for the *Neue Bach Ausgabe* (NBA), suggest that there may well have been others, now lost, a proposition rejected by Werner Breig in a more recent article on the Bach Suites (in: *The Cambridge Companion to Bach*, 1997, p133). Of the four survivors, only sets of parts (some in Bach's hand) and some copyists' scores are extant, the original autograph scores having disappeared. It would seem that we owe a good deal of our limited knowledge of the Suites Nos. 2, 3 and 4 to the diligence of Christian Friedrich Penzel (1737–1801) who was a student at the Thomasschule from 1751 (the year after Bach's death) and who made copies of Bach manuscripts he found there.

Thus, neither the dates nor the order of composition of the suites can be established with any certainty. The NBA editors suggest that they were composed in the order by which we know them today with the following approximate dates: No. 1 (BWV 1066) 1718, No. 2 (BWV 1067) 1721, No. 3 (BWV 1068) 1722, and No. 4 (BWV 1069) 1723. This would place the suites (or 'Ouverturen' as Bach called them), like the Brandenburg Concertos, in the composer's Cöthen period at which time No. 4 lacked the trumpets and timpani which were added in Leipzig at Christmas 1725 when the first movement was adapted for the opening chorus of the Cantata BWV 110, *Unser Mund sei voll Lachens*. It is possible that the trumpet parts and timpani of the Suite No. 3 were also added later in Leipzig but there is no direct evidence to support this. Breig even suggests that the Suite No. 3 may originally have been written for strings only (CD-liner-notes: Hyperion CDD22002, 1991).

An alternative and quite different chronology for these works is proposed by Stephen Daw, placing the Suite No. 3 in its original version first in order of composition 'by 1724' and the fourth suite in its first version, and the Suite No. 1, 'by the end of 1724', the final version of No. 4 being completed 'c.1729', and the Suite No. 3 'adapted to form its final version' between 'c.1729–31'. '[…] we have no evidence to indicate – as has often been stated –', writes Daw, 'that any of these works were composed before Bach's arrival in Leipzig in May 1723'. Breig supports this possibility and points out that all the surviving sources for the suites originated in Leipzig and proposes the following chronology: 'The principal source of Suite No. 1 […] almost certainly dates from his first year in office; in its original form, Suite No. 4 […] must have been completed before Christmas 1725; Suite No. 3 […] survives in a set of parts dating from 1731; and Suite No. 2 […] survives in an MS from around 1738/9.'

Overture (Suite) No. 1 in C major, BWV 1046

Composed: probably in Cöthen in ca. 1718, but in any case before 1725
Original publisher: not published during the composer's lifetime
Instrumentation: 2 oboes, bassoon – violin1 and 2, viola, violoncello,
double bass – continuo
Duration: ca. 22 minutes

Our present edition is based on three sources labelled A, B and C in the NBA Critical Report of 1967. Source A (orchestral parts: shelf-mark *Mus. ms. Bach St 152*) initialled C.G.M. by the copyist (identified as Christian Gottlob Messner). Sources B and C are MS scores with the shelf-marks *Am.B.551* and *Am.B.52*. All of these sources are located in the Staatsbibliothek zu Berlin – Preußischer Kulturbesitz, Musikabteilung mit Mendelssohn Archiv.

Overture (Suite) No. 2 in F major, BWV 1047

Composed: ca. 1721 in Cöthen, or later (see text)
Original publisher: not published during the composer's lifetime
Instrumentation: flute – violin 1 and 2, viola, violoncello, double bass –
continuo
Duration: ca. 19 minutes

The present Suite No. 2 (to which Stephen Daw allocates the dates 1737–39), is, he claims, 'almost certainly Bach's latest preserved example of this genre, although it is possible that the surviving set of Leipzig parts, with flute and viola in the hand of Bach himself, is copied from an earlier score, or one which had been adapted from a lost earlier version. However, on stylistic and other, historical, grounds it seems improbable that this popular suite was composed before the 1730s, and the actual use of the flute in the music would even in 1737 or later, have been up-to-date even in Paris.'

Irving Godt, in an article 'Politics, Patriotism and a Polonaise: A Possible Revision in Bach's Suite in B Minor' (*The Musical Quarterly*, 75, 1990) also suggests the period around 1735–36 for the reworking of the suite from an earlier (Cöthen?) version, possibly for Pierre-Gabriel Buffardin, the principal flautist of the Dresden Court Orchestra (a suggestion of Martin Bernstein, in: *Report of the Eigth Congress of the International Musicological Society*, 1962). At the same time he may well have added the Polonaise, a dance he rarely used but which he incorporated here in support of, or in thanks for, the granting of his petition for the title of composer-at-large to Augustus III, King of Poland and Elector of Saxony.

The main sources for our new edition are, inevitably, the above-mentioned MS materials which are preserved in the Staatsbibliothek zu Berlin – Preußischer Kulturbesitz, Musik-abteilung mit Mendelssohn-Archiv, copies of which we gratefully acknowledge. The most important of these are listed 'Sources A–G' in the NBA Critical Report, pp. 34–41, the most valuable of them being Source A, a set of MS parts two of which – Flute, headed 'Traversiere', and Viola – are in Bach's hand, the remaining parts being in the hands of four unidentified copyists with corrections by Bach. The library shelf-mark is *Mus. ms Bach St 154 (1–6)*. The cover bears the inscription 'H moll, Ouverture a 1 Flauto, 2 Violini, Viola e Baßo di J. S. Bach', and at the bottom of the page, in the later hand of Carl Friedrich Zelter (1758–1832), the incipits of the overture marked 'Grave' and the main section marked 'fuga'. The set has two Continuo parts, one of which is figured.

The NBA Source G bears the same basic shelf-mark (*Mus. ms. Bach St 154 (7–12)*) and is another set of MS parts neatly written and all in one hand. This has phrasings in addition to those in Source a, an indication, perhaps, of a performing convention in which slurring was expected although not always specifically marked. I have not shown these in our score.

I have also re-examined the 1913 Eulenburg score of the Suite No. 2 (edited by Wilhelm Alt-mann) as well as the *NBA* score of 1966 and the sources B–F listed in the Critical Report of 1967, both with much benefit. Sources D and E (the copies made by Penzel at the Thomas-schule, possibly from the now lost autograph) do have a few textual differences from Source A. Source D is a score in the Staatsbibliothek zu Berlin, shelf-mark *Mus. ms. Bach P 1065*. Source F, a neatly written MS score is a later copy of Source D and is signed 'Anton Werner, 28 Mai 1839'; it was of little consequence in the preparation of this new edition.

Harry Newstone (adapted)

Vorwort

Vom Beginn des 17. Jahrhunderts bis zu dem Moment, als sich Johann Sebastian Bach der Orchestersuite zuwandte, hatten schon verschiedene Komponisten zur Entwicklung dieser Gattung beigetragen. Hier ist vor allem Johann Rosenmüller (um 1619–1684) zu nennen, ein Vorgänger Bachs an der Thomasschule in Leipzig. Er wurde dort 1642 stellvertretender Kantor und veröffentlichte drei Jahre später sein erstes Werk – eine Sammlung von instrumentalen Tänzen mit dem Titel *Paduanen, Alemanden, Couranten, Balletten, Sarabanden mit 3 Stimmen und ihren Basso pro Organo*.

Aber auch andere deutsche Komponisten komponierten instrumentale Tanzsuiten; so z. B. Johann Caspar Fischer (um 1665–1746), dessen Opus 1 *Le Journal de printemps* (8 Ouvertüren-Suiten) 1695 gedruckt wurde, und später Georg Philipp Telemann (1681–1767) sowie Johann Friedrich Fasch (1688–1758). Fasch, ein Schüler von Bachs unmittelbarem Vorgänger Johann Kuhnau (1660–1722), schrieb eine Anzahl von Orchestersuiten, in denen er seinem Vorbild Telemann nacheiferte. Bei ihm ist aber auch, wie bei so vielen seiner zeitgenössischen, deutschen Komponistenkollegen, die meisterhafte Präsenz von Jean-Baptiste Lully (1632–1687) erkennbar. Diese zeigt sich nicht zuletzt in der Neuerung, den Tanzsätzen eine imposante 'Ouvertüre' voranzustellen, von der diese Form möglicherweise auch ihren Namen hat. Fasch, der später in die Dienste des Grafen Morzin zu Lukawitz in Böhmen trat (desjenigen Grafen also, der 1759 Joseph Haydn seine erste Musikdirektorenstelle gab), wurde von Bach, der mehrere seiner Orchestersuiten abschrieb, sehr bewundert.

Von Bach selbst sind nur vier Orchestersuiten überliefert. Heinrich Besseler, der diese Werke zusammen mit Hans Grüss in der Neuen Bach Ausgabe (NBA) edierte, vermutete allerdings, dass es möglicherweise mehr Werke gegeben habe, die nun aber verschollen seien. Diese These wurde jedoch von Werner Breig in einem Artikel über Bachs Suiten zurückgewiesen (in: *The Cambridge Companion to Bach*, 1997, S. 133). Von den vier überlieferten Werken existieren lediglich Stimmen (einige davon in Bachs Handschrift) sowie einige Partituren, die von Kopisten stammen. Die autographen Partituren sind verschollen. Ein Großteil unseres ohnehin begrenzten Wissens über die Suiten Nr. 2, 3 und 4 scheinen wir dem Eifer Christian Friedrich Penzels (1737–1801) zu verdanken. Er war seit 1751 (dem Jahr nach Bachs Tod) Schüler an der Thomasschule und kopierte die dort von ihm vorgefundenen Manuskripte Bachs.

Deshalb können wir weder über die Entstehungsdaten noch die Kompositionsreihenfolge gesicherte Aussagen machen. Die Herausgeber der NBA vertreten die These, dass sie in der uns heute bekannten Folge komponiert wurden, wobei sie hinsichtlich der Datierung von den folgenden Annäherungswerten ausgingen: Nr. 1 (BWV 1066) 1718, Nr. 2 (BWV 1067) 1721, Nr. 3 (BWV 1068) 1722, Nr. 4 (BWV 1069) 1723. Damit würden die Entstehungszeiten der Suiten (oder „Ouvertüren", wie sie Bach nannte), den Brandenburgischen Konzerten vergleichbar, noch in Bachs Köthener Zeit fallen. Zu diesem Zeitpunkt fehlten in der 4. Suite noch die Trompeten und Pauken. Sie wurden erst Weihnachten 1725 in Leipzig ergänzt, als Bach den ersten Satz für den Eröffnungschor der Kantate BWV 110 *Unser Mund sei voller Lachens* umarbeitete. Es ist ferner möglich, dass auch die Trompeten und Pauken der 3. Suite erst in der Leipziger Zeit ergänzt wurden, doch lassen sich dafür keine direkten Hinweise finden. Breig vermutet sogar, die 3. Suite sei ursprünglich nur für Streicher geschrieben worden (CD-Einführung: Hyperion CDD22002, 1991).

Eine gänzlich davon abweichende Chronologie schlägt Stephen Daw vor: Er setzt die 3. Suite in der Originalfassung als erste der vier Suiten „um 1724" an und die 4. Suite in ihrer ersten Fassung sowie die 1. Suite „gegen Ende 1724". Die Endfassung der 4. Suite sei „ca. 1729" beendet worden und die 3. Suite in ihrer endgültigen Form zwischen „ca. 1729 und 1731". Daws schreibt ferner: „[...] wir haben keinen Beweis dafür, dass – wie oft gesagt wurde – irgendeines dieser Werk vor Bachs Ankunft in Leipzig im Mai 1723 geschrieben wurde." Breig unterstützt diese Hypothese und weist darauf hin, dass alle überlieferten Quellen zu den Orchestersuiten aus Leipzig stammen. Er schlägt folgende Chronologie vor: „Die Hauptquelle der 1. Suite stammt mit ziemlicher Sicherheit aus seinem ersten Jahr in Leipzig. Die 4. Suite muß in ihrer Originalfassung vor Weihnachten 1725 beendet worden sein, die 3. Suite ist in einem Satz Orchesterstimmen von 1731 erhalten, und die 2. Suite ist in einem Manuskript aus dem Jahr 1738/39 überliefert."

Ouvertüre (Suite) Nr. 1 in C-Dur, BWV 1066

komponiert: wahrscheinlich Köthen um 1718, jedenfalls aber vor 1725
Originalverlag: zu Lebzeiten des Komponisten nicht gedruckt
Orchesterbesetzung: 2 Oboen, Fagott – Violine I und II, Viola, Violoncello,
Kontrabass – Basso continuo
Spieldauer: etwa 22 Minuten

Unsere vorliegende Edition basiert auf drei Quellen, die im Kritischen Bericht der NBA von 1967 als A, B und C gelistet werden. Quelle A (Orchesterstimmen: Signatur *Mus. ms. Bach St 152*) ist vom Kopisten mit C.G.M. unterzeichnet (er wurde als Christian Gottlob Messner identifiziert). Die Quellen B und C sind handschriftliche Quellen mit den Signaturen *Am.B.551* und *Am.B.52*. Sie befinden sich alle in der Staatsbibliothek zu Berlin – Preußischer Kulturbesitz, Musikabteilung mit Mendelssohn Archiv.

Ouvertüre (Suite) Nr. 2 in F-Dur, BWV 1067

komponiert: um 1721 in Köthen oder später (siehe unten)
Originalverlag: zu Lebzeiten des Komponisten nicht gedruckt
Orchesterbesetzung: Flöte – Violine I und II, Viola, Violoncello,
Kontrabass – Basso continuo
Spieldauer: etwa 19 Minuten

Von der vorliegenden 2. Suite, die er mit 1737–1739 datierte, meint Daw, sie sei „ziemlich sicher Bachs letztes erhaltenes Beispiel dieser Gattung, auch wenn es möglich ist, dass das überlieferte Leipziger Stimmenmaterial – dessen Flöten- und Violastimme Bach selbst schrieb – von einer älteren Partitur kopiert wurde oder von einer Bearbeitung einer früheren, verloren gegangenen Fassung. Aus stilistischen und anderen historischen Gründen scheint es jedenfalls unwahrscheinlich, dass diese bekannte Suite vor 1730 komponiert wurde, und die fortschrittliche Verwendung der Flöte wäre auch noch 1737 oder später selbst in Paris hochaktuell gewesen."

Irving Godt schlägt in seinem Artikel *Politics, Patriotism and a Polonaise: A Possible Revision in Bach's Suite in B Minor (The Musical Quarterly,* 75, 1990) für die Überarbeitung einer vielleicht aus der Köthener Zeit stammenden Frühfassung der Suite ebenfalls einen Zeitraum um 1735/36 vor. Martin Bernstein meint, dass sie möglicherweise für Pierre-Gabriel Buffardin, den ersten Flötisten des Dresdener Hoforchesters, erstellt wurde (in: *Report of the Eigth Congress of the International Musicological Society,* 1962). Bei dieser Gelegenheit könnte Bach die Polonaise hinzugefügt haben. Er hat diese Tanzart selten verwendet, aber sie hier wohl zur Unterstützung seines Gesuchs um Beförderung oder zum Dank für seine Ernennung zum „Kgl. Polnischen und Kurfürstl. Sächsischen Hofcompositeur, Kapellmeister und Director Chori musici in Leipzig" am Hof von August III., König von Polen und Kurfürst von Sachsen eingefügt.

Hauptquellen der vorliegenden Neuausgabe sind zwangsläufig die oben erwähnten Handschriften, die in der Staatsbibliothek zu Berlin – Preußischer Kulturbesitz, Musikabteilung mit Mendelssohn-Archiv, aufbewahrt werden. Für die Überlassung von Kopien sei ihr an dieser Stelle gedankt. Im Kritischen Bericht der NBA sind die wichtigsten Quellen unter den Kürzeln A–G auf den Seiten 34–41 beschrieben. Die wertvollste ist die Quelle A, ein handschriftlicher Stimmensatz, der zwei Stimmen (die mit „Traversiere" überschriebene Flöte und die Viola) von der Hand Bachs aufweist, während die anderen von vier bisher nicht identifizierten Kopisten geschrieben worden sind, aber Korrektureintragungen von Bach enthalten. Sie hat die Signatur: *Mus. ms. Bach St 154 (1–6).* Das Umschlagblatt trägt den Titel *H moll | Ouverture | a | 1 Flauto | 2 Violini | Viola | e | Baßo | di J. S: Bach.* Am Fuße der Seite hat später Carl Friedrich Zelter (1758–1832) die Incipits der Ouvertüre (mit *Grave* bezeichnet) und des Hauptthemas (mit *Fuga* bezeichnet) notiert. Der Satz enthält zwei Continuo-Stimmen, von denen eine ausgesetzt ist.

Die in der NBA als G bezeichnete Stimme hat die gleiche Grundsignatur: *Mus. ms. Bach St 154 (7–12).* Es handelt sich dabei um einen weiteren Stimmensatz, der in akurater Handschrift von lediglich einem Schreiber angefertigt wurde. Er weist gegenüber Quelle A zusätzliche Phrasierungen auf, was möglicherweise ein Indiz für eine Aufführungspraxis ist, in der Bindungen zwar erwartet, aber nicht immer speziell bezeichnet wurden. In der vorliegenden Partitur sind diese Zusätze nicht angezeigt.

Mit viel Gewinn habe ich auch nochmals die 1913 von Wilhelm Altmann herausgegebene Eulenburg-Partitur der 2. Suite sowie die NBA aus dem Jahre 1966 und die im dazugehörigen Kritischen Bericht von 1967 verzeichneten Quellen B–F untersucht. Quelle D und E (Abschriften, die Penzel in der Thomasschule vermutlich vom verschollenen Autograph herstellte) weisen einige Abweichungen von Quelle A auf. Quelle D ist eine Partitur aus dem Besitz der Staatsbibliothek zu Berlin (Signatur: *Mus ms. Bach P 1065*). Quelle F, eine sauber geschriebene handschriftliche Partitur, ist eine spätere Kopie der Quelle D und mit *Anton Werner, 28 Mai 1839* signiert. Für die Edition dieser Neuausgabe war sie nur von geringfügigem Wert.

Harry Newstone (neu bearbeitet)
Übersetzung: Ann-Katrin Heimer

Overture No. 1 in C major

Johann Sebastian Bach
(1685–1750)
BWV 1066

I. Ouverture

EAS 113

© 2006 Ernst Eulenburg Ltd, London
and Ernst Eulenburg & Co GmbH, Mainz

2

4

8

12

II. Courante

III. Gavotte 1 alternativement

Gavotte 2

Gavotte 1 da capo

IV. Forlane

V. Menuet 1 alternativement

Menuet 2

Menuet 1 da capo

VI. Bourrée 1 alternativement

22

Bourrée 2

Oboe

Fagotto

Ob.

Fg.

Ob.

Fg.

Ob.

Fg.

Ob.

Fg.

Bourrée 1 da capo

VII. Passepied 1 alternativement

24

Passepied 2

Oboe $\frac{1}{2}$

Violino I, II
Viola

Fagotto
Basso Continuo

p

6

Ob. $\frac{1}{2}$

Vl. I, II
Vla.

Fg.
B. c.

11

Ob. $\frac{1}{2}$

Vl. I, II
Vla.

Fg.
B. c.

17

Ob. $\frac{1}{2}$

Vl. I, II
Vla.

Fg.
B. c.

23

Ob. $\frac{1}{2}$

Vl. I, II
Vla.

Fg.
B. c.

Passepied 1 da capo

Overture No. 2 in B minor

Johann Sebastian Bach
(1685–1750)
BWV 1067

I. Ouverture

EAS 113

32

38

II. Rondeaux

III. Sarabande

IV. Bourrée I alternativement

44

II

Bourrée I da capo

V. Polonoise

Lentement

Flauto traverso

Violino I

Violino II

Viola

Basso continuo

moderato e staccato

Double

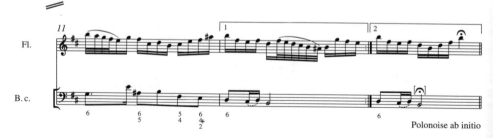

Polonoise ab initio

VI. Menuet

VII. Battinerie

Printed in China

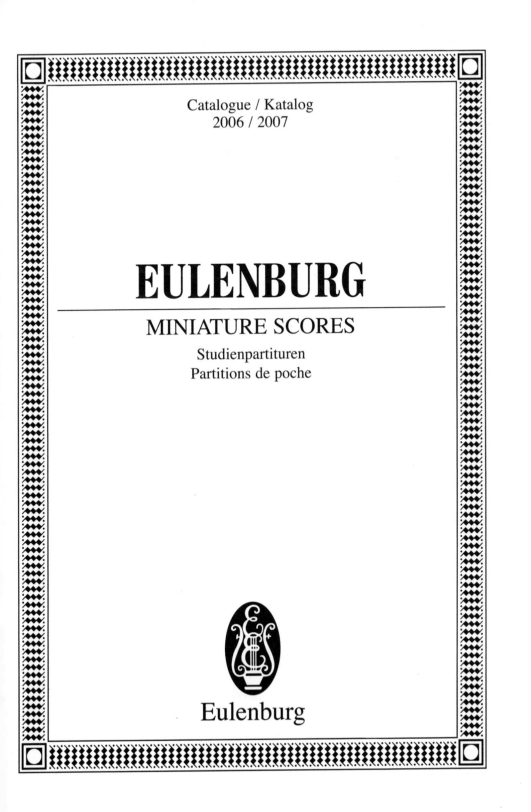

Albinoni, Tommaso
(1671-1750)

Magnificat
(Schroeder) [12']
study score
ISBN 3-7957-6180-8
ISMN M-2002-0916-7
ETP 1074
set of string parts
ISMN M-2002-2003-2
EOS 1074-50
wind band parts
ISMN M-2002-2001-8
EOS 1074-60
basso continuo
ISMN M-2002-2002-5
EOS 1074-65

Arne, Thomas Augustine
(1710-1778)

Thomas and Sally
Dramatic Pastoral in Two Acts
(Fiske)
ISMN M-2002-0789-7
ETP 926

Auber, Daniel François Esprit
(1782-1871)

Le Cheval de Bronze
(The bronze Horse / Das eherne Pferd)
Overture to the Opera
ISMN M-2002-0565-7
ETP 651

Le Domino noir
(The black Domino / Der schwarze Domino)
Overture to the Comic Opera
ISMN M-2002-0572-5
ETP 658

La Muette de Portici
(The Dumb Girl of Portici /
Die Stumme von Portici)
Overture to the Opera
ISMN M-2002-0594-7
ETP 689

Bach, Carl Philipp Emanuel
(1714-1788)

Choral and Vocal Works

Die Israeliten in der Wüste
(The Israelites in the Wilderness)
Oratorio, H 775 (Darvas)
ISMN M-2002-1085-9
ETP 1359

Magnificat
D major, H 772 (Darvas)
ISBN 3-7957-6966-3   ISMN M-2002-1084-2
ETP 1358

Concertos

Concerto A minor
for harpsichord or flute or cello and strings
H 430-32 (Altmann)
study score
ISBN 3-7957-7116-1   ISMN M-2002-0683-8
ETP 781
solo parts:
flute
ISMN M-2002-1285-3
PC 21-02
cello
ISMN M-2002-1284-6
PC 21-01
harpsichord
ISMN M-2002-1286-0
PC 21-03
separate parts:
violin I
ISMN M-2002-1287-7
PC 21-11
violin II
ISMN M-2002-1288-4
PC 21-12
viola
ISMN M-2002-1289-1
PC 21-13
cello/double bass
ISMN M-2002-1290-7
PC 21-14
basso continuo
ISMN M-2002-1291-4
PC 21-15

Concerto A major
for flute or cello or harpsichord, strings and
basso continuo, H 437-39,
Wq 168, 172, 29 (Kneihs)
study score
ISBN 3-7957-6107-7   ISMN M-2002-1013-2
ETP 1259
solo parts:
flute
ISMN M-2002-1674-5
PC 94-01

cello
ISMN M-2002-1675-2
PC 94-02
harpsichord/piano
ISMN M-2002-1676-9
PC 94-03
separate parts:
violin I
ISMN M-2002-1678-3
PC 94-12
violin II
ISMN M-2002-1679-0
PC 94-13
viola
ISMN M-2002-1680-6
PC 94-14
cello/double basses rip.
ISMN M-2002-1681-3
PC 94-15
basso continuo
ISMN M-2002-1677-6
PC 94-11

Bach, Johann Christian
(1735-1782)

Orchestral Works

Symphony G minor, op. 6/6
(Platt)
ISMN M-2002-0516-9
ETP 596   (L)

Symphony E♭ major, op. 9/2
(Stein)
study score
ISBN 3-7957-6351-7   ISMN M-2002-0447-6
ETP 522
wind band parts
(2 oboes or flutes, 2 horns)
ISMN M-2002-1219-8
PC 7-10
separate parts:
violin I
ISMN M-2002-1220-4
PC 7-11
violin II
ISMN M-2002-1221-1
PC 7-12
viola
ISMN M-2002-1222-8
PC 7-13
cello/double bass
ISMN M-2002-1223-5
PC 7-14
harpsichord
ISMN M-2002-1224-2
PC 7-15
oboe I/flute I
EOS 522-16

e II/flute II
522-17

n I
522-18

n II
522-19

n I
522-11

n II
522-12

a
522-13

/double bass
522-14

so continuo
522-65

mphony B♭ major, op. 18/2
echey)
N 3-7957-6736-9   ISMN M-2002-0515-2
595

mphony D major, op. 18/4
stein)

dy score
N 3-7957-6359-2   ISMN M-2002-0446-9
521

d band parts
lutes, 2 oboes, bassoon, 2 horns in d,
umpets, timpani)
N M-2002-1225-9
3-10

arate parts:
n I
N M-2002-1227-3
3-12

n II
N M-2002-1228-0
3-13

a
N M-2002-1229-7
3-14

/double bass
N M-2002-1230-3
3-15

psichord
N M-2002-1226-6
3-11

ncertos

fonia concertante A major
violin, cello and orchestra (Einstein)

dy score
N 3-7957-6796-2   ISMN M-2002-0666-1
765

o parts:
n
N M-2002-1231-0
9-01

o
N M-2002-1232-7
9-02

---

wind band parts (2 oboes, 2 horns)
ISMN M-2002-1233-4
PC 9-10

separate parts:
violin I rip.
ISMN M-2002-1235-8
PC 9-12

violin II rip.
ISMN M-2002-1236-5
PC 9-13

viola
ISMN M-2002-1237-2
PC 9-14

cello/double basses rip.
ISMN M-2002-1238-9
PC 9-15

harpsichord
ISMN M-2002-1234-1
PC 9-11

Sinfonia Concertante E♭ major
for 2 violins and orchestra (Stein)

study score
ISMN M-2002-0669-2
ETP 768

solo parts:
violin I
ISMN M-2002-1191-7
PC 1-01

violin II
ISMN M-2002-1192-4
PC 1-02

wind band parts
(2 flutes, 2 oboes, 2 horns)
ISMN M-2002-1193-1
PC 1-10

separate parts:
violin I
ISMN M-2002-1194-8
PC 1-11

violin II
ISMN M-2002-1195-5
PC 1-12

viola
ISMN M-2002-1196-2
PC 1-13

cello/double bass
ISMN M-2002-1197-9
PC 1-14

harpsichord
ISMN M-2002-1198-6
PC 1-15

Sinfonia concertante C major
for flute, oboe, violin, cello and orchestra
ISMN M-2002-0993-8
ETP 1236   (L)

Sinfonia concertante F major
for oboe, cello and orchestra (Dawes)

study score
ISBN 3-7957-7135-8   ISMN M-2002-1019-4
ETP 1265

solo cello
EOS 1265-01

---

separate parts:
oboe I
EOS 1265-24

oboe II
EOS 1265-25

violin I
EOS 1265-11

violin II
EOS 1265-12

viola
EOS 1265-13

cello/double bass
EOS 1265-14

horn I/II
EOS 1265-21

Concerto E♭ major
for harpsichord and strings (Praetorius)

study score
ISMN M-2002-0674-6
ETP 773

solo harpsichord
ISMN M-2002-1255-6
PC 14-01

separate parts:
violin I
ISMN M-2002-1256-3
PC 14-11

violin II
ISMN M-2002-1257-0
PC 14-12

viola
ISMN M-2002-1258-7
PC 14-13

cello/double bass
ISMN M-2002-1259-4
PC 14-14

Bach, Johann Sebastian
(1685-1750)
Choral and Vocal Works

Johannes-Passion
(St John Passion) BWV 245 (Schering)
ISBN 3-7957-6121-2   ISMN M-2002-0813-9
ETP 965

Matthäus-Passion
(St Matthew Passion) BWV 244 (Grischkat)
ISBN 3-7957-6200-6   ISMN M-2002-0802-3
ETP 953

Magnificat D major
BWV 243 (Schering)
ISBN 3-7957-6628-1   ISMN M-2002-0812-2
ETP 964

Hohe Messe in h-Moll
BWV 232 (Volbach)
ISBN 3-7957-6201-4   ISMN M-2002-0806-1
ETP 959

Weihnachtsoratorium
(Christmas Oratorio), BWV 248 (Schering)
ISBN 3-7957-6276-6   ISMN M-2002-0810-8
ETP 962

Singet dem Herrn ein neues Lied
Motette Nr. 1 aus Psalm 149 und 150
BWV 225 (Stein)
ISMN M-2002-0878-8
ETP 1035

Cantatas / Kantaten

Christ lag in Todesbanden
BWV 4 (1724) (Schering)
ISBN 3-7957-6890-X   ISMN M-2002-0855-9
ETP 1011

Bleib bei uns,
denn es will Abend werden
Feria 2 Paschatos, BWV 6 (Grischkat)
ISBN 3-7957-6198-0   ISMN M-2002-0848-1
ETP 1004

Christ, unser Herr, zum Jordan kam
Festo S. Joannis Baptistae, BWV 7 (Schering)
ISMN M-2002-0882-5
ETP 1039

Liebster Gott, wann werd ich sterben
Dominica 16 post Trinitatis, BWV 8 (Schering)
ISMN M-2002-0871-9
ETP 1028

Lobet Gott in seinen Reichen
Himmelfahrtsoratorium (1735), BWV 11
(Schering)
ISMN M-2002-0846-7
ETP 1002

Weinen, Klagen, Sorgen, Zagen
Dominica Jubilate, BWV 12 (Horn)
ISBN 3-7957-6183-2   ISMN M-2002-0845-0
ETP 1001

Wer Dank opfert, der preiset mich
Dominica 14 post Trinitatis, BWV 17 (Grischkat)
ISMN M-2002-0901-3
ETP 1058

Es erhub sich ein Streit
Festo Michaelis (1726), BWV 19 (Schering)
ISMN M-2002-0870-2
ETP 1027

Ich hatte viel Bekümmernis
Dominica Palmarum, BWV 21 (Schering)
ISBN 3-7957-6319-3   ISMN M-2002-0872-6
ETP 1029

Du wahrer Gott und Davids Sohn
Dominica Esto mihi, BWV 23 (Grischkat)
ISBN 3-7957-6260-X   ISMN M-2002-0890-0
ETP 1047

Wer weiß, wie nahe mir mein Ende
Dominica 16 post Trinitatis, BWV 27 (Grischkat)
ISMN M-2002-0892-4
ETP 1049

Gottlob! nun geht das Jahr zu Ende
auf den Sonntage nach Weihnachten, BWV 28
(Grischkat)
ISMN M-2002-0927-3
ETP 1085

Wir danken dir, Gott
Ratswahl-Kantate (1731), BWV 29 (Grischkat)
ISBN 3-7957-6202-2   ISMN M-2002-0900-6
ETP 1057

Liebster Jesu, mein Verlangen
Dominica 1 post Epiphanias, BWV 32
ISBN 3-7957-6181-6   ISMN M-2002-0895-5
ETP 1052

O ewiges Feuer, o Ursprung der Liebe
Festo Pentecostes, BWV 34 (Schering)
ISMN M-2002-0857-3
ETP 1013

Aus tiefer Not schrei ich zu dir
Dominica 21 post Trinitatis, BWV 38 (Grischkat)
ISBN 3-7957-6177-8   ISMN M-2002-0909-9
ETP 1066

Brich dem Hungrigen dein Brot
Dominica 1 post Trinitatis, BWV 39 (Schering)
ISBN 3-7957-6193-X   ISMN M-2002-0879-5
ETP 1036

Schauet doch und sehet
Dominica 10 post Trinitatis, BWV 46 (Schering)
ISMN M-2002-0868-9
ETP 1025

Nun ist das Heil und die Kraft
BWV 50 (Schering)
ISMN M-2002-0861-0
ETP 1018

Jauchzet Gott in allen Landen
Dominica 15 post Trinitatis et in ogni Tempo
BWV 51 (Schering)
ISBN 3-7957-6254-5   ISMN M-2002-0881-8
ETP 1038

Schlage doch, gewünschte Stunde
Trauermusik, BWV 53
ISMN M-2002-0887-0
ETP 1044

Ich armer Mensch, ich Sündenknecht
Dominica 22 post Trinitatis, BWV 55 (Schering)
ISMN M-2002-0864-1
ETP 1021

Ich will den Kreuzstab gerne tragen
Kreuzstab-Kantate; Dominica 19 post Trinitatis,
BWV 56 (Schering)
ISBN 3-7957-6244-8   ISMN M-2002-0852-8
ETP 1008

Nun komm, der Heiden Heiland
Adventus Christi (1. Fassung), BWV 61
(Grischkat)
ISBN 3-7957-6227-8   ISMN M-2002-0889-4
ETP 1046

Nun komm, der Heiden Heiland
Adventus Christi (2. Fassung), BWV 62
(Grischkat)
ISBN 3-7957-6329-0   ISMN M-2002-0891-7
ETP 1048

Halt im Gedächtnis Jesum Christ
Dominica Quasimodogeniti (1725), BWV 67
(Schering)
ISMN M-2002-0885-6
ETP 1042

Also hat Gott die Welt geliebt
Feria 2 Pentecostes, BWV 68 (Grischkat)
ISBN 3-7957-6149-2   ISMN M-2002-0898-6
ETP 1055

Jesu, der du meine Seele
Dominica 14 post Trinitatis (1740), BWV 78
(Schering)
ISBN 3-7957-6145-X   ISMN M-2002-0874-0
ETP 1031

Gott, der Herr, ist Sonn' und Schild
Festo Reformationis (1735), BWV 79 (Scher
ISBN 3-7957-6207-3   ISMN M-2002-0853-5
ETP 1009

Ein' feste Burg ist unser Gott
Reformationskantate (1730), BWV 80
(Schering)
ISBN 3-7957-6301-0   ISMN M-2002-0847-4
ETP 1003

Jesus schläft, was soll ich hoffen?
Dominica 4 post Epiphanias (1724), BWV 81
(Schering)
ISMN M-2002-0858-0
ETP 1014

Ich hab in Gottes Herz und Sinn
Dominica Septuagesimae, BWV 92 (Schering)
ISMN M-2002-0876-4
ETP 1033

Nimm von uns, Herr, du treuer Gott
Dominica 10 post Trinitatis, BWV 101
(Grischkat)
ISMN M-2002-0921-1
ETP 1079

Du Hirte Israel, höre
Am Sonntage Misericordias Domini (1725),
BWV 104 (Grischkat)
ISBN 3-7957-6767-9   ISMN M-2002-0866-5
ETP 1023

Gottes Zeit ist die allerbeste Zeit
Actus tragicus, BWV 106 (Schering)
ISBN 3-7957-6302-9   ISMN M-2002-0851-1
ETP 1007

Der Herr ist mein getreuer Hirt
BWV 112
ISMN M-2002-0922-8
ETP 1080

Sei Lob und Ehr' dem höchsten Gut
BWV 117 (Grischkat)
ISBN 3-7957-6199-9   ISMN M-2002-0919-8
ETP 1077

eise, Jerusalem, den Herrn
V 119 (Schering)
N 3-7957-6958-2 ISMN M-2002-0873-3
1030

rr Jesu Christ,
hr'r Mensch und Gott
ninica Estomihi, BWV 127 (Grischkat)
IN M-2002-0908-2
1065

s der Tiefe rufe ich, Herr, zu dir
Im 130, BWV 131 (Grischkat)
N 3-7957-6248-0 ISMN M-2002-0894-8
1051

be den Herren,
n mächtigen König der Ehren
ninica 12 post Trinitatis, BWV 137
ischkat)
N 3-7957-6123-9 ISMN M-2002-0902-0
1059

chet auf, ruft uns die Stimme
nenica 27 post Trinitatis (1731), BWV 140
hering)
N 3-7957-6769-5 ISMN M-2002-0863-4
1020

in Gott, wie lang, ach lange
ninica 2 post Epiphanias, BWV 155
hering)
IN M-2002-0877-1
1034

r Friede sei mit dir
atate zum 3. Ostertag, BWV 158 (Grischkat)
N 3-7957-6315-0 ISMN M-2002-0893-1
1050

het, wir gehn hinauf gen Jerusalem
ninica Estomihi (1729), BWV 159 (Grischkat)
IN M-2002-0899-3
1056

mm, du süße Todesstunde
ninica 16 post Trinitatis, BWV 161 (Horn)
IN M-2002-0849-8
1005

ist ein trotzig und verzagt Ding
sto Trinitatis, BWV 176 (Schering)
IN M-2002-0875-7
1032

he zu, dass deine Gottesfurcht nicht
uchelei sei
ninica 11 post Trinitatis, BWV 179
ischkat)
IN M-2002-0917-4
1075

mmelskönig, sei willkommen
ninica Palmarum, BWV 182 (Schering)
N 3-7957-6988-4 ISMN M-2002-0867-2
1024

hweigt stille, plaudert nicht
fee-Kantate, BWV 211 (Schering)
N 3-7957-6297-9 ISMN M-2002-0880-1
1037

Mer hahn en neue Oberkeet
Bauern-Kantate, BWV 212 (Alberti)
ISBN 3-7957-6270-7 ISMN M-2002-0850-4
ETP 1006

Zerreißet, zersprenget,
zertrümmert die Gruft
Der zufriedengestellte Aeolus, BWV 205
(Schering)
ISBN 3-7957-7145-5 ISMN M-2002-0815-3
ETP 967

Orchestral Works
Overtures (Suites)
No. 1 C major, BWV 1066
(Altmann)
ISBN 3-7957-6789-X ISMN M-2002-0738-5
ETP 856

No. 2 B minor, BWV 1067
(Newstone)
ISBN 3-7957-6842-X ISMN M-2002-0717-0
ETP 821

No. 3 D major, BWV 1068
(Newstone)
ISBN 3-7957-6669-9 ISMN M-2002-0716-3
ETP 818

No. 4 D major, BWV 1069
(Altmann)
ISBN 3-7957-6354-1 ISMN M-2002-0742-2
ETP 861

Concertos
Brandenburg Concertos
No. 1 F major, BWV 1046
for 2 horns, 3 oboes, bassoon, strings and
basso continuo (Stöckl)
ISBN 3-7957-6196-4 ISMN M-2002-0255-7
ETP 280

No. 2 F major, BWV 1047
for flute, oboe, trumpet, violin, strings and
basso continuo (Stöckl)
ISBN 3-7957-6265-0 ISMN M-2002-0237-3
ETP 257

No. 3 G major, BWV 1048
for string orchestra (Stöckl)
ISBN 3-7957-6126-3 ISMN M-2002-0235-9
ETP 254

No. 4 G major, BWV 1049
for violin principal, 2 flutes and strings (Fiske)
ISBN 3-7957-6723-7 ISMN M-2002-0257-1
ETP 281

No. 5 D major, BWV 1050
for flute, violin, harpsichord concertante and
strings (Stöckl)
ISBN 3-7957-6188-3 ISMN M-2002-0258-8
ETP 282

No. 6 Bb major, BWV 1051
for 2 viola da braccio, 2 viola da gamba, cello
and basso continuo (Stöckl)
ISBN 3-7957-6328-2 ISMN M-2002-0236-6
ETP 255

Concerto D minor
for harpsichord and strings, BWV 1052
(Schering)
ISMN M-2002-0645-6
ETP 744

Concerto F minor
for harpsichord and strings, BWV 1056
(Schering)
ISBN 3-7957-6922-1 ISMN M-2002-0646-3
ETP 745

Concerto C major
for 2 harpsichords and strings, BWV 1061
(Schering)
ISBN 3-7957-7117-X ISMN M-2002-0632-6
ETP 730

Concerto C minor
after the lost concerto for 2 violins or oboe and
violin, BWV 1060
for 2 harpsichords and strings (Schering)
ISBN 3-7957-6900-0 ISMN M-2002-0633-3
ETP 731

Concerto D minor
after the lost concerto for violin, flute and oboe,
BWV 1063
for 3 harpsichords and strings (Schering)
ISMN M-2002-0634-0
ETP 732

Concerto C major
for 3 harpsichords and strings, BWV 1064
(Schering)
ISMN M-2002-0635-7
ETP 733

Concerto A minor
after the concerto for 4 violins op. 3/10
by Vivaldi
for 4 harpsichords and strings, BWV 1065
(Schering)
ISMN M-2002-0660-9
ETP 759

Concerto A minor
for violin, strings and basso continuo,
BWV 1041 (Pfarr)
ISBN 3-7957-6197-2 ISMN M-2002-0613-5
ETP 711

Concerto E major
for violin, strings and basso continuo,
BWV 1042 (Schering)
ISBN 3-7957-6253-7 ISMN M-2002-0614-2
ETP 712

Double Concerto D minor
for 2 violins and orchestra, BWV 1043
ISBN 3-7957-6809-8 ISMN M-2002-0629-6
ETP 727

Triple Concerto A minor
for harpsichord, flute, violin and strings, BWV
1044 (Schering)
ISBN 3-7957-6755-5 ISMN M-2002-0658-6
ETP 757

Chamber Music

Die Kunst der Fuge
(Art of Fugue) (1749-50), BWV 1080 (Williams)
ISBN 3-7957-6747-4   ISMN M-2002-1112-2
ETP 1391

Musikalisches Opfer
(Musical Offering), BWV 1079 (Williams)
ISMN M-2002-1111-5
ETP 1390

Balakirev, Mily Alexayevich
(1837-1910)

Tamara
Symphonic Poem (Lloyd-Jones)
ISMN M-2002-0518-3
ETP 598

Barsanti, Franco
(c. 1690 - c. 1776)

Concerto grosso D major
for strings, 2 french horns and timpani, op. 3/4
study score
ISMN M-2002-0677-7
ETP 776
wind band parts (2 horns, timpani)
ISMN M-2002-1260-0
PC 15-10
separate parts:
violin I
ISMN M-2002-1261-7
PC 15-11
violin II
ISMN M-2002-1262-4
PC 15-12
viola
ISMN M-2002-1263-1
PC 15-13
cello/double bass
ISMN M-2002-1264-8
PC 15-14
harpsichord
ISMN M-2002-1265-5
PC 15-15

Beethoven, Ludwig van
(1770-1827)

Opera

Fidelio, op. 72
ISBN 3-7957-6192-1   ISMN M-2002-0780-4
ETP 914

Choral and Vocal Works

Missa C major
op. 86 (Hess)
ISBN 3-7957-6190-5   ISMN M-2002-0840-5
ETP 996

Missa solemnis
D major, op. 123 (Hess)
ISBN 3-7957-6120-4   ISMN M-2002-0801-6
ETP 951

Chor-Fantasie
C minor, op. 80
for piano, chorus and orchestra (Hess)
ISBN 3-7957-6646-X   ISMN M-2002-1065-1
ETP 1333

Ah, perfido!
Scena and Aria, op. 65
for soprano and orchestra (Unger)
ISMN M-2002-0886-3
ETP 1043

Egmont
Musik zu Goethes Trauerspiel
for soprano and orchestra (Altmann)
ISBN 3-7957-6946-9   ISMN M-2002-0719-4
ETP 823

Orchestral Works

Symphonies
(Unger)

No. 1 C major, op. 21
ISBN 3-7957-6875-6   ISMN M-2002-0355-4
ETP 418

No. 2 D major, op. 36
ISBN 3-7957-6854-3   ISMN M-2002-0356-1
ETP 419

No. 3 E♭ major, op. 55
"Eroica"
ISBN 3-7957-6639-7   ISMN M-2002-0342-4
ETP 405

No. 4 B♭ major, op. 60
ISBN 3-7957-6178-6   ISMN M-2002-0351-6
ETP 414

No. 5 C minor, op. 67
ISBN 3-7957-6618-4   ISMN M-2002-0339-4
ETP 402

No. 6 F major, op. 68
"Pastorale"
ISBN 3-7957-6846-2   ISMN M-2002-0344-8
ETP 407

No. 7 A major, op. 92
ISMN M-2002-0349-3
ETP 412

No. 8 F major, op. 93
ISMN M-2002-0353-0
ETP 416

No. 9 D minor, op. 125
"Choral"
ISBN 3-7957-6779-2   ISMN M-2002-0348-6
ETP 411

Wellingtons Sieg oder die Schlacht bei Vittoria, op. 91
(Wellington's Victory or the Battle of Vittoria)
„Schlachtensinfonie" (Küthen)
ISBN 3-7957-6249-9   ISMN M-2002-1092-7
ETP 1367

Overtures
(Unger)

Prometheus, op. 43
to the Ballet "Die Geschöpfe des Prometheus"
ISBN 3-7957-6793-8   ISMN M-2002-0545-9
ETP 625

Coriolan, op. 62
ISBN 3-7957-6623-0   ISMN M-2002-0546-6
ETP 626

Leonore
Overture No. 1 to "Fidelio", op. 138
ISBN 3-7957-6760-1   ISMN M-2002-0548-0
ETP 628

Overture No. 2 to "Fidelio", op. 72
ISBN 3-7957-7101-3   ISMN M-2002-0549-7
ETP 629

Overture No. 3 to "Fidelio"
ISBN 3-7957-6719-9   ISMN M-2002-0521-3
ETP 601

Fidelio, op. 72b
ISBN 3-7957-6609-5   ISMN M-2002-0530-5
ETP 610

Egmont, op. 84
ISBN 3-7957-6662-1   ISMN M-2002-0524-4
ETP 604

Die Ruinen von Athen, op. 113
(The Ruins of Athens)
ISBN 3-7957-6610-9   ISMN M-2002-0550-3
ETP 630

Große Ouvertüre C-Dur
Zur Namensfeier, op. 115
ISMN M-2002-0552-7
ETP 632

König Stephan, op. 117
ISBN 3-7957-6976-0   ISMN M-2002-0551-0
ETP 631

Die Weihe des Hauses, op. 124
(The Consecration of the House)
ISMN M-2002-0547-3
ETP 627

Concertos

Concerto No. 1 C major
for piano and orchestra, op. 15
including all cadences written by the compos[er]
himself (Altmann)
ISBN 3-7957-6686-9   ISMN M-2002-0626-5
ETP 724

oncerto No. 2 B♭ major
piano and orchestra, op. 19
luding all cadences written by the composer
nself (Altmann)
3N 3-7957-6643-5   ISMN M-2002-0627-2
P 725

oncerto No. 3 C minor
piano and orchestra, op. 37   (Altmann)
3N 3-7957-6665-6   ISMN M-2002-0606-7
P 704

oncerto No. 4 G major
piano and orchestra, op. 58   (Altmann)
3N 3-7957-6622-2   ISMN M-2002-0607-4
P 705

oncerto No. 5 E♭ major
mperor"
piano and orchestra, op. 73
adura-Skoda/Imai)
BN 3-7957-6155-7   ISMN M-2002-0608-1
P 706

oncerto E♭ major
piano and orchestra, WoO 4
:luding all cadences written by the composer
nself (Hess)
3N 3-7957-6303-7   ISMN M-2002-1034-7
P 1281

oncerto D major
violin and orchestra, op. 61   (Tyson)
3N 3-7957-6887-X   ISMN M-2002-0603-6
P 701

iple Concerto C major
piano, violin, cello and orchestra, op. 56
3N 3-7957-6688-5   ISMN M-2002-0631-9
P 729

Romances G major and ⎿ major
violin and orchestra, op. 40 / op. 50
3N 3-7957-6903-5   ISMN M-2002-0704-0
P 803

hamber Music

tring Trio E♭ major, op. 3
ske/Platen)
BN 3-7957-6942-6   ISMN M-2002-0063-8
P 41

tring Trio D major, op. 8
erenade
BN 3-7957-6920-5   ISMN M-2002-0067-6
P 45

tring Trio G major, op. 9/1
ltmann)
BN 3-7957-6677-X   ISMN M-2002-0064-5
P 42

tring Trio D major, op. 9/2
ltmann)
BN 3-7957-6611-7   ISMN M-2002-0065-2
P 43

tring Trio C minor, op. 9/3
tmann)
BN 3-7957-6751-2   ISMN M-2002-0066-9
P 44

String Quartets
(Altmann)
F major, op. 18/1
"Amenda" (final version)
ISBN 3-7957-6788-1   ISMN M-2002-0039-3
ETP 16

G major, op. 18/2
"Komplimentier"
ISBN 3-7957-6839-X   ISMN M-2002-0040-9
ETP 17

D major, op. 18/3
ISMN M-2002-0041-6
ETP 18

C minor, op. 18/4
ISBN 3-7957-6634-6   ISMN M-2002-0042-3
ETP 19

A major, op. 18/5
ISBN 3-7957-6291-X   ISMN M-2002-0043-0
ETP 20

B♭ major, op. 18/6
"La Malinconia"
ISBN 3-7957-7128-5   ISMN M-2002-0044-7
ETP 21

"Rasumovsky" Quartets
F major, op. 59/1
ISBN 3-7957-6331-2   ISMN M-2002-0050-8
ETP 28

E minor, op. 59/2
ISBN 3-7957-6953-1   ISMN M-2002-0051-5
ETP 29

C major, op. 59/3
ISBN 3-7957-6817-9   ISMN M-2002-0052-2
ETP 30

E♭ major, op. 74
"Harp Quartet" / "Harfen-Quartett"
ISBN 3-7957-6856-X   ISMN M-2002-0045-4
ETP 22

F minor, op. 95
"Quartetto serioso"
ISBN 3-7957-6971-X   ISMN M-2002-0037-9
ETP 14

E♭ major, op. 127
ISBN 3-7957-6945-0   ISMN M-2002-0058-4
ETP 36

B♭ major, op. 130
ISBN 3-7957-6756-3   ISMN M-2002-0032-4
ETP 9

C minor, op. 131
ISBN 3-7957-6803-9   ISMN M-2002-0026-3
ETP 2

A minor, op. 132
"Thanksgiving" / "Dankgesang"
ISBN 3-7957-6732-6   ISMN M-2002-0029-4
ETP 6

B♭ major, op. 133
"Grand Fugue" / "Große Fuge"
ISBN 3-7957-6944-2   ISMN M-2002-0118-5
ETP 98

F major, op. 135
"The difficult resolve" /
"Der schwergefasste Entschluss"
ISBN 3-7957-6853-5   ISMN M-2002-0028-7
ETP 4

F major, op. 14/1
arranged by the composer
from piano sonata E major
ISBN 3-7957-6349-5   ISMN M-2002-0266-3
ETP 297

Quintet E♭ major
for 2 violins, 2 violas and cello, op. 4
ISBN 3-7957-6347-9   ISMN M-2002-0209-0
ETP 214

Quintet-Fugue D major
for 2 violins, 2 violas and cello, op. 137 (1817)
ISMN M-2002-0210-6
ETP 216

Piano Trios
No. 1 E♭ major, op. 1/1
ISMN M-2002-0139-0
ETP 122

No. 2 G major, op. 1/2
ISBN 3-7957-6879-9   ISMN M-2002-0140-6
ETP 123

No. 3 C minor, op. 1/3
ISMN M-2002-0141-3
ETP 124

No. 4 B♭ major, op. 11
for piano, clarinet (or violin) and cello (1798)
ISBN 3-7957-6812-8   ISMN M-2002-0214-4
ETP 223

No. 5 D major, op. 70/1
"Geister-Trio" (1808)
ISBN 3-7957-6635-4   ISMN M-2002-0102-4
ETP 82

No. 6 E♭ major, op. 70/2
ISMN M-2002-0103-1
ETP 83

No. 7 B♭ major, op. 97
"Archduke" / "Erzherzog-Trio" (1811)
ISBN 3-7957-6820-9   ISMN M-2002-0099-7
ETP 79

No. 11 G major, op. 121a
"Kakadu Variations" (1803)
ISMN M-2002-0254-0
ETP 278

Piano Quartet E♭ major, op. 16
arranged by the composer from piano quintet
ISMN M-2002-0133-8
ETP 114

Trio C major, op. 87
for 2 oboes and cor anglais
ISBN 3-7957-6981-7 ISMN M-2002-0124-6
ETP 104

Sextet E♭ major, op. 71
for 2 clarinets, 2 bassoons and 2 horns
ISMN M-2002-0145-1
ETP 139

Octet E♭ major, op. 103
for 2 oboes, 2 clarinets, 2 bassoons and 2 horns
(Altmann)
ISBN 3-7957-7106-4 ISMN M-2002-0144-4
ETP 135

Rondino E♭ majeur
for 2 oboes, 2 clarinets, 2 bassoons and 2 horns
op. posth., WoO 25
ISMN M-2002-0234-2
ETP 252

Trio G major
for piano, flute and bassoon, WoO 37
ISBN 3-7957-6612-5 ISMN M-2002-0335-6
ETP 397

Quintet E♭ major, op. 16
for piano, oboe, clarinet, horn and bassoon
ISBN 3-7957-6772-5 ISMN M-2002-0204-5
ETP 200

Serenade D major, op. 25
for flute, violin and viola
ISBN 3-7957-6743-1 ISMN M-2002-0123-9
ETP 103

Sextet E♭ major, op. 81b
for 2 violins, viola, cello and 2 horns
ISBN 3-7957-6899-3 ISMN M-2002-0146-8
ETP 140

Septet E♭ major, op. 20
for violin, viola, cello, double bass, clarinet,
horn and bassoon
ISBN 3-7957-6648-6 ISMN M-2002-0035-5
ETP 12

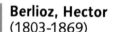

Berlioz, Hector
(1803-1869)

Choral and Vocal Works

Requiem
Grande messe des morts, op. 5
ISMN M-2002-1168-9
ETP 8003

Les Nuits d'Eté
op. 7 (Fiske)
ISBN 3-7957-6822-5 ISMN M-2002-0930-3
ETP 1093

La Damnation de Faust
Dramatic Legend in four Parts, op. 24
ISBN 3-7957-7126-9 ISMN M-2002-0838-2
ETP 994

L'Enfance du Christ
op. 25 (Fiske)
ISBN 3-7957-6749-0 ISMN M-2002-0929-7
ETP 1092

Orchestral Works

Symphonie Fantastique
from Hector Berlioz New Edition of the
Complete Works Vol. 16 (Temperley)
ISBN 3-7957-6629-X ISMN M-2002-0359-2
ETP 422

Harold en Italie
Symphony for viola and orchestra, op. 16 (1834)
(Bruno)
ISBN 3-7957-6333-9 ISMN M-2002-0360-8
ETP 423

Roméo et Juliette
Dramatic Symphony, op. 17
ISBN 3-7957-7112-9 ISMN M-2002-0361-5
ETP 424

Waverley
Overture, op. 1 (Fiske)
ISBN 3-7957-6325-8 ISMN M-2002-0537-4
ETP 617

Les Francs Juges, op. 3
(The Judges of the secret Court /
Die Vehmrichter) – Overture
ISMN M-2002-0538-1
ETP 618

Roi Lear, op. 4
Overture
ISMN M-2002-0539-8
ETP 619

Le carnaval romain, op. 9
Overture
ISBN 3-7957-6717-2 ISMN M-2002-0540-4
ETP 620

Le Corsaire, op. 21
(The Corsair / Der Korsar)
Overture (MacDonald)
ISMN M-2002-0541-1
ETP 621

Benvenuto Cellini, op. 23
Overture to the Opera
ISMN M-2002-0542-8
ETP 622

Chasse Royale et Orage
(Royal Hunt and Storm /
Königliche Jagd und Sturm)
from "Les Troyens" (MacDonald)
ISMN M-2002-1096-5
ETP 1371

La damnation de Faust, op. 24
3 orchestral pieces
ISMN M-2002-0702-6
ETP 801

Bizet, Georges
(1838-1875)

Opera

Carmen
Opéra comique in 4 acts (1873-75) (Didion)
ISBN 3-7957-6311-8 ISMN M-2002-2055-1
ETP 8062   (L)

Orchestral Works

Symphony C major
(Schönzeler)
ISBN 3-7957-7100-5 ISMN M-2002-0476-6
ETP 556

L'Arlésienne Suite No. 1
study score
ISBN 3-7957-6823-3 ISMN M-2002-0723-1
ETP 828

wind band parts
ISMN M-2002-2037-7
EOS 828-60

set of string parts
(6 violins I, 5 violins II, 4 violas, 5 cellos,
2 double basses)
ISMN M-2002-1992-0
EOS 828-50

separate parts:
violin I
ISMN M-2002-1988-3
EOS 828-11
violin II
ISMN M-2002-1989-0
EOS 828-12
viola
ISMN M-2002-1990-6
EOS 828-13
cello
ISMN M-2002-1991-3
EOS 828-14
double bass
ISMN M-2002-1993-7
EOS 828-15

L'Arlésienne Suite No. 2
study score
ISBN 3-7957-6941-8 ISMN M-2002-0724-8
ETP 829

wind band parts
ISMN M-2002-2044-5
EOS 829-60

set of string parts
(6 violins I, 5 violins II, 4 violas, 5 cellos,
2 double basses)
ISMN M-2002-2043-8
EOS 829-50

separate parts:
violin I
ISMN M-2002-2038-4
EOS 829-11
violin II
ISMN M-2002-2039-1
EOS 829-12

a
ISMN M-2002-2040-7
829-13

o
ISMN M-2002-2041-4
829-14

ble bass
ISMN M-2002-2042-1
829-15

ux d'Enfants
ite suite d'orchestre, op. 22
N 3-7957-7121-8   ISMN M-2002-0766-8
898

oma
certo Suite No. 3
ISMN M-2002-0727-9
832

Bloch, Ernest
(1880-1959)

mphony C minor
ISMN M-2002-1813-8
8030

Blow, John (1649-1708)

de for St. Cecilia's Day 1691
ISMN M-2002-0915-0
1073

Boccherini, Luigi
(1743-1805)

oncertos

ello Concerto B♭ major
482 (Sturzenegger)
udy score
ISMN M-2002-0681-4
780

lo cello
ISMN M-2002-1305-8
24-01

parate parts:
rn I
ISMN M-2002-1306-5
24-11
rn II
ISMN M-2002-1307-2
24-12
lin I
ISMN M-2002-1308-9
24-13
lin II
ISMN M-2002-1309-6
24-14

---

viola
ISMN M-2002-1310-2
PC 24-15
cello/double bass
ISMN M-2002-1311-9
PC 24-16

Chamber Music

Serenade D major
for 2 oboes, 2 horns, 2 violins and b.c. (Haas)
study score
ISMN M-2002-0312-7
ETP 373
wind band parts
ISMN M-2002-1369-0
PC 41-10
separate parts:
violin I
ISMN M-2002-1370-6
PC 41-11
violin II
ISMN M-2002-1371-3
PC 41-12
cello/double bass
ISMN M-2002-1372-0
PC 41-13
harpsichord
ISMN M-2002-1373-7
PC 41-14

Boieldieu, Francois Adrien
(1775-1834)

Le Calife de Bagdad
(Der Kalif von Bagdad)
Overture to the Comic Opera (Cauchie)
ISBN 3-7957-6996-5   ISMN M-2002-0940-2
ETP 1105

La Dame Blanche
(The white Lady / Die weiße Dame)
Overture to the Comic Opera
ISMN M-2002-0564-0
ETP 650

Borodin, Alexander
(1833-1887)

String Quartet No. 2 D major
(Brown)
ISBN 3-7957-6651-6   ISMN M-2002-0205-2
ETP 201

Symphony No. 1 E♭ major
ISMN M-2002-0421-6
ETP 490

Symphony No. 2 B minor
ISBN 3-7957-6659-1   ISMN M-2002-0422-3
ETP 491

Symphony No. 3 A minor
"Unfinished" (Lloyd-Jones)
ISBN 3-7957-6282-0   ISMN M-2002-0428-5
ETP 501

In the Steppes of Central Asia
(Eine Steppenskizze aus Mittelasien)
ISBN 3-7957-6606-0   ISMN M-2002-0728-6
ETP 833

Polovtsian Dances
(Polowetzer Tänze)
from the Opera "Prince Igor"
ISBN 3-7957-7111-0   ISMN M-2002-0759-0
ETP 886

Prince Igor
Overture
ISBN 3-7957-6763-6   ISMN M-2002-0951-8
ETP 1118

Boyce, William
(1710-1779)

Orchestral Works

8 Symphonies, op. 2
(Platt)
study score
ISMN M-2002-1138-2
ETP 1527
score (= basso continuo)
ISMN M-2002-1840-4
EOS 1527-65
wind band parts
ISMN M-2002-1839-8
EOS 1527-60
set of string parts
ISMN M-2002-1841-1
EOS 1527-70
separate parts:
violin I
ISMN M-2002-1835-0
EOS 1527-11
violin II
ISMN M-2002-1836-7
EOS 1527-12
viola
ISMN M-2002-1837-4
EOS 1527-13
basso
ISMN M-2002-1838-1
EOS 1527-14

Concertos

Concerto grosso E minor
for 2 violins, cello and string orchestra
(Platt)
study score
ISMN M-2002-1025-5
ETP 1271
solo parts:
violin I
ISMN M-2002-1754-4
PC 109-01
violin II
ISMN M-2002-1755-1
PC 109-02
cello
ISMN M-2002-1756-8
PC 109-03
separate parts:
violin I rip.
ISMN M-2002-1757-5
PC 109-11
violin II rip.
ISMN M-2002-1758-2
PC 109-12
viola
ISMN M-2002-1759-9
PC 109-13
cello rip.
ISMN M-2002-1760-5
PC 109-14
harpsichord
ISMN M-2002-1761-2
PC 109-15

Concerto grosso B minor
for 2 violins, cello and string orchestra
(Beechey)
study score
ISMN M-2002-1028-6
ETP 1274
solo parts:
violin I
ISMN M-2002-1762-9
PC 110-01
violin II
ISMN M-2002-1763-6
PC 110-02
cello
ISMN M-2002-1764-3
PC 110-03
separate parts:
violin I rip.
ISMN M-2002-1765-0
PC 110-11
violin II rip.
ISMN M-2002-1766-7
PC 110-12
viola
ISMN M-2002-1767-4
PC 110-13
cello rip.
ISMN M-2002-1768-1
PC 110-14

organ
ISMN M-2002-1769-8
PC 110-15

Concerto grosso B♭ major
for 2 violins, cello and string orcherstra
(Beechey)
study score
ISMN M-2002-1029-3
ETP 1275
solo parts:
violin I
EOS 1275-01
violin II
EOS 1275-02
cello
EOS 1275-03
separate parts:
violin I
EOS 1275-11
violin II
EOS 1275-12
viola
EOS 1275-13
cello/double bass
EOS 1275-16
basso continuo
EOS 1275-65

Brahms, Johannes

(1833-1897)

Choral and Vocal Works

Ein deutsches Requiem
(A German Requiem)
nach Worten der Heiligen Schrift, op. 45
ISMN M-2002-0816-0
ETP 969

Rhapsody
for alto, male chorus and orchestra, op. 53
ISBN 3-7957-6744-X   ISMN M-2002-0897-9
ETP 1054

Schicksalslied
(Song of Destiny), op. 54
for choir and orchestra (Chissell)
ISBN 3-7957-6364-9   ISMN M-2002-1139-9
ETP 1601

Orchestral Works

Symphonies
(Altmann)
No. 1 C minor, op. 68
ISBN 3-7957-6682-6   ISMN M-2002-0362-2
ETP 425

No. 2 D major, op. 73
ISBN 3-7957-6701-6   ISMN M-2002-0363-9
ETP 426

No. 3 F major, op. 90
ISBN 3-7957-6654-0   ISMN M-2002-0364-6
ETP 427

No. 4 E minor, op. 98
ISBN 3-7957-6640-0   ISMN M-2002-0365-3
ETP 428

Akademische Fest-Ouvertüre, op. 80
(Academic Festival Overture) (Fiske)
ISBN 3-7957-6753-9   ISMN M-2002-0570-1
ETP 656

Tragische Ouvertüre, op. 81
(Tragic Overture) (Altmann)
ISBN 3-7957-6913-2   ISMN M-2002-0571-8
ETP 657

Variationen über ein Thema vc Joseph Haydn, op. 56a
(Variations on a Theme of Haydn)
ISMN M-2002-0706-4
ETP 805

Serenade for Orchestra D major, op. 11
ISBN 3-7957-6139-5   ISMN M-2002-0737-8
ETP 855

Serenade for Orchestra A major, op. 16
ISBN 3-7957-6330-4   ISMN M-2002-0743-9
ETP 862

Concertos

Piano Concerto No. 1 D minor
op. 15 (Badura-Skoda)
ISBN 3-7957-6716-4   ISMN M-2002-0615-9
ETP 713

Piano Concerto No. 2 B major
op. 83 (Altmann)
ISBN 3-7957-6733-4   ISMN M-2002-0617-3
ETP 715

Violin Concerto D major
op. 77 (Altmann)
ISBN 3-7957-6770-9   ISMN M-2002-0618-0
ETP 716

Double Concerto A minor
for violin, cello and orchestra, op. 102
ISBN 3-7957-7103-X   ISMN M-2002-0625-8
ETP 723

Chamber Music

String Quartet C minor
op. 51/1 (Altmann)
ISBN 3-7957-6961-2   ISMN M-2002-0222-9
ETP 240

String Quartet A minor
op. 51/2 (Altmann)
ISBN 3-7957-6652-4   ISMN M-2002-0223-6
ETP 241

String Quartet B♭ major
op. 67 (Altmann)
ISBN 3-7957-6874-8   ISMN M-2002-0224-3
ETP 242

tring Quintet F major
violins, 2 violas and cello, op. 88
(tmann)
BN 3-7957-6161-1   ISMN M-2002-0219-9
P 237

tring Quintet G major
2 violins, 2 violas and cello, op. 111
(tmann)
BN 3-7957-6934-5   ISMN M-2002-0220-5
P 238

tring Sextet B♭ major
2 violins, 2 violas and 2 cellos, op. 18
BN 3-7957-6680-X   ISMN M-2002-0217-5
P 235

tring Sextet G major
2 violins, 2 violas and 2 cellos, op. 36 (1860)
(tmann)
BN 3-7957-7125-0   ISMN M-2002-0218-2
P 236

iano Trio B major, op. 8
BN 3-7957-6935-3   ISMN M-2002-0228-1
P 246

iano Trio C major, op. 87
BN 3-7957-6910-8   ISMN M-2002-0229-8
P 247

iano Trio C minor, op. 101
MN M-2002-0230-4
P 248

iano Quartet G minor, op. 25
BN 3-7957-6932-9   ISMN M-2002-0225-0
P 243

iano Quartet A major
. 26 (Altmann)
MN M-2002-0226-7
P 244

iano Quartet C minor
. 60 (Altmann)
BN 3-7957-6332-0   ISMN M-2002-0227-4
P 245

iano Quintet F minor
. 34 (Altmann)
BN 3-7957-6206-5   ISMN M-2002-0208-3
P 212

uintet B minor
clarinet and string quartet, op. 115
ranmer)
BN 3-7957-6681-8   ISMN M-2002-0221-2
P 239

iano Trio E♭ major
piano, violin and horn (or cello or viola),
. 40 (Altmann)
BN 3-7957-6616-8   ISMN M-2002-0231-1
P 249

rio A minor
piano, clarinet (viola) and cello, op. 114
BN 3-7957-6745-8   ISMN M-2002-0232-8
P 250

Bruch, Max
(1838-1920)

Violin Concerto No. 1 G minor
op. 26
ISBN 3-7957-6718-0   ISMN M-2002-0616-6
ETP 714

Bruckner, Anton

(1824-1896)

Choral and Vocal Works

Mass E minor
1882 Version (Nowak)
ISBN 3-7957-6118-2   ISMN M-2002-1849-7
ETP 1606

Mass No. 3 F minor
(Redlich)
(bound/Broschur)
ISBN 3-7957-6220-0   ISMN M-2002-0808-5
ETP 961
(imitation leather/Kunstleder)
ISMN M-2002-0809-2
ETP 961-01

Psalm 150
(Redlich)
ISBN 3-7957-6205-7   ISMN M-2002-0819-1
ETP 972

Te Deum
ISMN M-2002-0807-8
ETP 960

Orchestral Works

Symphonies
(Nowak = from Bruckner Complete Edition)
No. 0 D minor
1869 version "Nullte" (Nowak)
ISBN 3-7957-6117-4   ISMN M-2002-1848-0
ETP 1530

No. 1/1 C minor
1865/66 version "Linzer Fassung" (Nowak)
ISBN 3-7957-6113-1   ISMN M-2002-1844-2
ETP 459

No. 1/2 C minor
1890/91 version "Wiener Fassung" (Brosche)
ISBN 3-7957-6114-X   ISMN M-2002-1845-9
ETP 1522

No. 3/1 D minor
1873 version "Wagner-Symphony" (Nowak)
ISBN 3-7957-6122-0   ISMN M-2002-0396-7
ETP 461

No. 3/2 D minor
1877 version "Wagner-Symphony" (Nowak)
ISBN 3-7957-6115-8   ISMN M-2002-1846-6
ETP 1523

No. 3/3 D minor
1889 version "Wagner-Sympony" (Nowak)
ISBN 3-7957-6116-6   ISMN M-2002-1847-3
ETP 1524

No. 4/1 E♭ major
1874 version "Romantic" (Redlich)
ISMN M-2002-0397-4
ETP 462

No. 4/2 E♭ major
1878/80 version "Romantic" (Nowak)
ISMN M-2002-1817-6
ETP 1525

No. 5 B♭ major
(Nowak)
ISBN 3-7957-6791-1   ISMN M-2002-0398-1
ETP 463

No. 6 A major
(Nowak)
ISBN 3-7957-7139-0   ISMN M-2002-0399-8
ETP 464

No. 7 E major
(Redlich)
ISBN 3-7957-6956-6   ISMN M-2002-0400-1
ETP 465

No. 8/1 C minor
1887 version (Nowak)
ISMN M-2002-1809-1
ETP 466

No. 8/2 C minor
1890 version (Nowak)
ISMN M-2002-1810-7
ETP 1526

No. 9 D minor
(Nowak)
ISBN 3-7957-7113-7   ISMN M-2002-0401-8
ETP 467

Overture G minor
(Walker)
ISMN M-2002-0588-6
ETP 681

Chamber Music

String Quintet F major
for 2 violins, 2 violas and cello
ISBN 3-7957-6195-6   ISMN M-2002-0278-6
ETP 310

Butterworth, George
(1885-1916)

A Shropshire Lad
Rhapsody
ISMN M-2002-1103-0
ETP 1382

Byrd, William
(1543-1623)

Mass in F minor
ISBN 3-7957-6603-6   ISMN M-2002-0841-2
ETP 997

Mass in F major
ISBN 3-7957-6604-4   ISMN M-2002-0842-9
ETP 998

Mass in D minor
ISBN 3-7957-6802-0   ISMN M-2002-0843-6
ETP 999

Campra, André
(1660-1744)

Messe de Mort
study score
ISBN 3-7957-6907-8   ISMN M-2002-2053-7
ETP 8047

set of solo parts
ISMN M-2002-2060-5
EOS 8047-70

separate parts:
flute/violin
ISMN M-2002-2056-8
EOS 8047-16

hautes-contre de violon
ISMN M-2002-2057-5
EOS 8047-17

tailles de violon
ISMN M-2002-2058-2
EOS 8047-18

bass
ISMN M-2002-2059-9
EOS 8047-19

Chabrier, Alexis Emanuel
(1841-1894)

España
Rhapsody
ISMN M-2002-0762-0
ETP 893

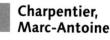

Charpentier, Marc-Antoine
(1643-1704)

Messe de Minuit
Weihnachtsmesse, H 9 (liturgisch)
(Montagnier)
study score
ISBN 3-7957-6714-8   ISMN M-2002-1820-6
ETP 8041

separate parts:
flute (recorder) I
ISMN M-2002-2263-0
EOS 8041-21

flute (recorder) II
ISMN M-2002-2264-7
EOS 8041-22

violin I
ISMN M-2002-2257-9
EOS 8041-11

violin II
ISMN M-2002-2258-6
EOS 8041-12

viola
ISMN M-2002-2259-3
EOS 8041-13

viola II
ISMN M-2002-2261-6
EOS 8041-16

cello
ISMN M-2002-2260-9
EOS 8041-14

basso continuo
ISMN M-2002-2262-3
EOS 8041-17

Te Deum
study score
ISBN 3-7957-6722-9   ISMN M-2002-1821-3
ETP 8042

separate parts:
flute I
ISMN M-2002-2271-5
EOS 8042-21

flute II
ISMN M-2002-2272-2
EOS 8042-22

oboe I
ISMN M-2002-2273-9
EOS 8042-23

oboe II
ISMN M-2002-2274-6
EOS 8042-24

trumpets I+II in C
ISMN M-2002-2275-3
EOS 8042-44

timpani
ISMN M-2002-2276-0
EOS 8042-64

violin I
ISMN M-2002-2265-4
EOS 8042-11

violin II
ISMN M-2002-2266-1
EOS 8042-12

viola I
ISMN M-2002-2267-8
EOS 8042-13

viola II
ISMN M-2002-2269-2
EOS 8042-16

cello
ISMN M-2002-2268-5
EOS 8042-14

basso continuo
ISMN M-2002-2270-8
EOS 8042-17

Chopin, Frédéric
(1810-1849)

Piano Concerto No. 1 E minor
ISBN 3-7957-6137-9   ISMN M-2002-0977-8
ETP 1215

Piano Concerto No. 2 F minor
ISBN 3-7957-6280-4   ISMN M-2002-0978-5
ETP 1216

Cimarosa, Domenico
(1749-1801)

Il Matrimonio segreto
(The secret Marriage / Die heimliche Ehe)
Overture to the Opera
ISMN M-2002-0944-0
ETP 1109

Corelli, Arcangelo
(1653-1713)

Concerti grossi, op. 6/1-12
(Platt)
study score (complete)
ISBN 3-7957-6726-1   ISMN M-2002-1891-6
ETP 1826-37

No. 1 D major
score (= basso continuo)
ISMN M-2002-1924-1
EOS 1826-65

set of string parts
ISMN M-2002-1925-8
EOS 1826-70

separate parts:
violin I
ISMN M-2002-1920-3
EOS 1826-11

violin II
ISMN M-2002-1921-0
EOS 1826-12

viola
ISMN M-2002-1922-7
EOS 1826-13

cello
ISMN M-2002-1923-4
EOS 1826-14

. 2 F major
ore (= basso continuo)
MN M-2002-1930-2
S 1827-65
t of string parts
MN M-2002-1931-9
S 1827-70
parate parts:
lin I
MN M-2002-1926-5
S 1827-11
lin II
MN M-2002-1927-2
S 1827-12
la
MN M-2002-1928-9
S 1827-13
lo
MN M-2002-1929-6
S 1827-14

. 3 C minor
ore (= basso continuo)
MN M-2002-1936-4
S 1828-65
t of string parts
MN M-2002-1937-1
S 1828-70
parate parts:
lin I
MN M-2002-1932-6
S 1828-11
lin II
MN M-2002-1933-3
S 1828-12
la
MN M-2002-1934-0
S 1828-13
lo
MN M-2002-1935-7
S 1828-14

. 4 D minor
ore (= basso continuo)
MN M-2002-1942-5
S 1829-65
t of string parts
MN M-2002-1943-2
S 1829-70
parate parts:
lin I
MN M-2002-1938-8
S 1829-11
lin II
MN M-2002-1939-5
S 1829-12
la
MN M-2002-1940-1
S 1829-13
lo
MN M-2002-1941-8
S 1829-14

No. 5 B♭ major
score (= basso continuo)
ISBN 3-7957-6933-7   ISMN M-2002-1948-7
EOS 1830-65
set of string parts
ISMN M-2002-1949-4
EOS 1830-70
separate parts:
violin I
ISMN M-2002-1944-9
EOS 1830-11
violin II
ISMN M-2002-1945-6
EOS 1830-12
viola
ISMN M-2002-1946-3
EOS 1830-13
cello
ISMN M-2002-1947-0
EOS 1830-14

No. 6 F major
score (= basso continuo)
ISMN M-2002-1954-8
EOS 1831-65
set of string parts
ISMN M-2002-1955-5
EOS 1831-70
separate parts:
violin I
ISMN M-2002-1950-0
EOS 1831-11
violin II
ISMN M-2002-1951-7
EOS 1831-12
viola
ISMN M-2002-1952-4
EOS 1831-13
cello
ISMN M-2002-1953-1
EOS 1831-14

No. 7 D major
score (= basso continuo)
ISMN M-2002-1960-9
EOS 1832-65
set of string parts
ISMN M-2002-1961-6
EOS 1832-70
separate parts:
violin I
ISMN M-2002-1956-2
EOS 1832-11
violin II
ISMN M-2002-1957-9
EOS 1832-12
viola
ISMN M-2002-1958-6
EOS 1832-13
cello
ISMN M-2002-1959-3
EOS 1832-14

No. 8 G minor
Christmas Concerto
study score
ISBN 3-7957-6724-5   ISMN M-2002-1892-3
ETP 1833
score (= basso continuo)
ISMN M-2002-1889-3
EOS 1833-65
set of string parts
ISMN M-2002-1890-9
EOS 1833-70
separate parts:
violin I solo/rip.
ISMN M-2002-1885-5
EOS 1833-11
violin II solo/rip.
ISMN M-2002-1886-2
EOS 1833-12
viola
ISMN M-2002-1887-9
EOS 1833-13
cello/double bass solo/rip.
ISMN M-2002-1888-6
EOS 1833-14

No. 9 F major
study score (Einstein)
ISMN M-2002-0303-5
ETP 359
score (= basso continuo)
(Platt)
ISMN M-2002-1966-1
EOS 1834-65
set of string parts
ISMN M-2002-1967-8
EOS 1834-70
separate parts:
violin I
ISMN M-2002-1962-3
EOS 1834-11
violin II
ISMN M-2002-1963-0
EOS 1834-12
viola
ISMN M-2002-1964-7
EOS 1834-13
cello
ISMN M-2002-1965-4
EOS 1834-14

No. 10 C major
score (= basso continuo)
ISMN M-2002-1972-2
EOS 1835-65
set of string parts
ISMN M-2002-1973-9
EOS 1835-70
separate parts:
violin I
ISMN M-2002-1968-5
EOS 1835-11
violin II
ISMN M-2002-1969-2
EOS 1835-12

viola
ISMN M-2002-1970-8
EOS 1835-13

cello
ISMN M-2002-1971-5
EOS 1835-14

No. 11 B♭ major
score (= basso continuo)
ISMN M-2002-1978-4
EOS 1836-65

set of string parts
ISMN M-2002-1979-1
EOS 1836-70

separate parts:
violin I
ISMN M-2002-1974-6
EOS 1836-11

violin II
ISMN M-2002-1975-3
EOS 1836-12

viola
ISMN M-2002-1976-0
EOS 1836-13

cello
ISMN M-2002-1977-7
EOS 1836-14

No. 12 F major
score (= basso continuo)
ISMN M-2002-1984-5
EOS 1837-65

set of string parts
ISMN M-2002-1985-2
EOS 1837-70

separate parts:
violin I
ISMN M-2002-1980-7
EOS 1837-11

violin II
ISMN M-2002-1981-4
EOS 1837-12

viola
ISMN M-2002-1982-1
EOS 1837-13

cello
ISMN M-2002-1983-8
EOS 1837-14

 Cornelius, Peter
(1824-1874)

Der Barbier von Bagdad
(The Barber of Bagdad)
Overture to the Opera
ISMN M-2002-0559-6
ETP 644

El Cid
Overture
ISMN M-2002-0560-2
ETP 645

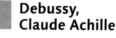 **Debussy,
Claude Achille**
(1862-1918)

La Mer
3 Symphonic Sketches
ISBN 3-7957-6187-5   ISMN M-2002-1058-3
ETP 1321

**Prélude à l'après-midi
d'un faune**
Eglogue pour Orchestre d'après Mallarmé
ISBN 3-7957-6134-4   ISMN M-2002-0950-1
ETP 1116

3 Nocturnes
ISMN M-2002-1057-6
ETP 1320

Images
(Fiske)
No. 1 Gigues
ISMN M-2002-1174-0
ETP 8009

No. 2 Iberia
ISBN 3-7957-6859-4   ISMN M-2002-1175-7
ETP 8010

No. 3 Rondes de printemps
ISMN M-2002-1811-4
ETP 8011

String Quartet G minor, op. 10
ISBN 3-7957-6313-4   ISMN M-2002-0207-6
ETP 210

**Dittersdorf,
Karl Ditters von**
(1739-1799)

String Quartet No. 2 B♭ major
ISMN M-2002-0126-0
ETP 107

**Dohnányi,
Ernst von**
(1877-1960)

Ruralia Hungarica
5 Pieces, op. 32b
ISMN M-2002-1069-9
ETP 1339

Symphonische Minuten
(Symphonic Minutes) op. 36
ISMN M-2002-1070-5
ETP 1340

Dvořák, Antonín
(1841-1904)

Orchestral Works

Symphonies
No. 4 D minor, op. 13, B 41
ISBN 3-7957-6225-1   ISMN M-2002-0513-8
ETP 593

No. 5 F major, op. 76, B 54
(früher Nr. 3)
ISBN 3-7957-6104-2   ISMN M-2002-0497-1
ETP 577

No. 6 D major, op. 60, B 112
ISBN 3-7957-6217-0   ISMN M-2002-0489-6
ETP 569

No. 7 D minor, op. 70, B 141
(früher Nr. 2)
ISBN 3-7957-6221-9   ISMN M-2002-0450-6
ETP 526

No. 8 G major, op. 88, B 163
(Döge)
ISBN 3-7957-6243-X   ISMN M-2002-0449-0
ETP 525

No. 9 E minor, op. 95, B 178
"From the New World" /
"Aus der Neuen Welt" (Döge)
ISBN 3-7957-6174-3   ISMN M-2002-0370-7
ETP 433

Symphonic Variations
op. 78, B 70 (Abraham)
ISBN 3-7957-7123-4   ISMN M-2002-1048-4
ETP 1304

Vodník, op. 107, B 195
(The Watersprite / Der Wassermann)
Symphonic Poem after K. Jaromir Erben
ISBN 3-7957-6108-5   ISMN M-2002-0507-7
ETP 587

Carnival
Overture, op. 92, B 169
ISBN 3-7957-6236-7   ISMN M-2002-0595-4
ETP 690

Scherzo capriccioso
op. 66, B 133 (B 131) (Swarowsky)
ISBN 3-7957-6929-9   ISMN M-2002-0752-1
ETP 873

Slavonic Dances
op. 46, Nos 1-4, B 83
ISBN 3-7957-6284-7   ISMN M-2002-1074-3
ETP 1346

op. 46, Nos 5-8, B 83
ISBN 3-7957-6259-6   ISMN M-2002-1075-0
ETP 1347

op. 72, Nos 1-4, B 147
ISBN 3-7957-6267-7   ISMN M-2002-1076-7
ETP 1348

72, Nos 5-8, B 147
N 3-7957-6250-2   ISMN M-2002-1077-4
1349

renade E major
strings, op. 22, B 52
N 3-7957-6335-5   ISMN M-2002-0764-4
896

ncertos

olin Concerto A minor
53, B 108 (Cherbuliez)
N 3-7957-6230-8   ISMN M-2002-0652-4
751

llo Concerto B minor
104, B 191 (Fiske)
N 3-7957-6691-5   ISMN M-2002-0686-9
785

amber Music

ring Quartets

minor, op. 34, B 75
N 3-7957-6172-7   ISMN M-2002-0267-0
298

major, op. 51, B 92
N 3-7957-6848-9   ISMN M-2002-0268-7
299

major, op. 61, B 121
N 3-7957-6843-8   ISMN M-2002-0269-4
300

najor, op. 80, B 57
N M-2002-0270-0
301

najor, op. 96, B 179
herican" / "Amerikanisches"
N 3-7957-6127-1   ISMN M-2002-0271-7
302

major, op. 105, B 193
N 3-7957-6350-9   ISMN M-2002-0272-4
303

najor, op. 106, B 192
N 3-7957-7142-0   ISMN M-2002-0273-1
304

ring Quintet G major
2 violins, viola, cello and double bass
77, B 49
N 3-7957-6695-8   ISMN M-2002-0291-5
338

ring Quintet E♭ majeur
2 violins, 2 violas and cello, op. 97, B 180
N 3-7957-6884-5   ISMN M-2002-0275-5
306

ring Sextet A major
2 violins, 2 violas and 2 cellos, op. 48, B 80
N 3-7957-6771-7   ISMN M-2002-0290-8
337

Piano Trio F minor
op. 65, B 130
ISMN M-2002-0287-8
ETP 331

Piano Trio E minor
"Dumky", op. 90, B 166
ISBN 3-7957-6947-7   ISMN M-2002-0288-5
ETP 332

Piano Quartet E♭ major
for piano, violin, viola and cello, op. 87, B 162
ISBN 3-7957-6974-4   ISMN M-2002-0286-1
ETP 330

Piano Quintet A major
for piano, 2 violins, viola and cello,
op. 81, B 155
ISBN 3-7957-6256-1   ISMN M-2002-0274-8
ETP 305

Serenade D minor
for 10 wind instruments, cello and
double bass, op. 44, B 77
ISBN 3-7957-6672-9   ISMN M-2002-1054-5
ETP 1314

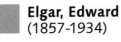

Elgar, Edward
(1857-1934)

Symphonies

No. 1 A♭ major, op. 55
ISMN M-2002-1170-2
ETP 8005

No. 2 E♭ major, op. 63
ISMN M-2002-1171-9
ETP 8006

Enigma-Variations
Variations on an Original Theme, op. 36
ISBN 3-7957-6710-5   ISMN M-2002-0757-6
ETP 884

Introduction and Allegro
for strings, op. 47
ISBN 3-7957-6889-6   ISMN M-2002-0758-3
ETP 885

Violin Concerto B minor
op. 61 (McVeagh)
ISBN 3-7957-6343-6   ISMN M-2002-1160-3
ETP 1817

Cello Concerto E minor
op. 85
ISBN 3-7957-6713-X   ISMN M-2002-1157-3
ETP 1814

Piano Quintet A minor
op. 84
ISBN 3-7957-6928-0   ISMN M-2002-0336-3
ETP 399

Fauré, Gabriel
(1845-1924)

Choral and Vocal Works

Requiem, op. 48
ISMN M-2002-0932-7
ETP 1096

Pavane, op. 50
for orchestra with chorus (ad lib.)
(1886) (Orledge)
ISBN 3-7957-7130-7   ISMN M-2002-1104-7
ETP 1383

Orchestral Works

Masques et Bergamasques
Suite, op. 112 (Orledge)
ISBN 3-7957-6904-3   ISMN M-2002-1108-5
ETP 1387

Pelléas et Mélisande
Suite, op. 80 (Orledge)
ISBN 3-7957-7133-1   ISMN M-2002-1107-8
ETP 1386

Concertos

Ballade
for piano and orchestra, op. 19 (Orledge)
ISMN M-2002-1105-4
ETP 1384

Elégie
for cello and orchestra, op. 24 (Orledge)
ISMN M-2002-1106-1
ETP 1385

Chamber Music

Piano Quartet No. 1
op. 15 (Orledge)
ISBN 3-7957-6712-1   ISMN M-2002-1124-5
ETP 1403

Piano Quartet No. 2
op. 45 (Orledge)
ISBN 3-7957-6949-3   ISMN M-2002-1125-2
ETP 1404

Franck, César
(1822-1890)

Orchestral Works

Symphony D minor
ISBN 3-7957-6828-4   ISMN M-2002-0414-8
ETP 482

Le chasseur maudit
Symphonic Poem (Coeuroy)
ISMN M-2002-0441-4
ETP 514

Rédemption
Symphonic Poem (Coeuroy)
ISMN M-2002-0448-3
ETP 523

Symphonic Variations
for piano and orchestra (Cauchie)
ISBN 3-7957-6774-1   ISMN M-2002-0639-5
ETP 738

Chamber Music

String Quartet D major
ISBN 3-7957-6991-4   ISMN M-2002-0284-7
ETP 323

Piano Trio F minor, op. 1/1
ISMN M-2002-0304-2
ETP 360

Piano Quintet F minor
ISBN 3-7957-6777-6   ISMN M-2002-0285-4
ETP 329

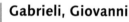

Gabrieli, Giovanni

(1557-1612)

In exclesiis
Motette a 15 (Hudson)
study score
ISMN M-2002-0904-4
ETP 1061

separate parts:
trumpet I/violin I
ISMN M-2002-1594-6
PC 79-11

trumpet II/violin II
ISMN M-2002-1595-3
PC 79-12

trumpet III/violin III
ISMN M-2002-1596-0
PC 79-13

trombone I/viola
ISMN M-2002-1597-7
PC 79-14

trombone II/cello I
ISMN M-2002-1598-4
PC 79-15

trombone III/cello II
ISMN M-2002-1599-1
PC 79-16

organ
ISMN M-2002-1600-4
PC 79-17

Geminiani, Francesco

(c. 1687-1762)

Concerti grossi, op. 3
for string quartet and string orchestra
(Hernried)

No. 1 D major
study score
ISMN M-2002-0305-9
ETP 361

separate parts:
violin I solo/rip.
ISMN M-2002-1199-3
PC 3-11

violin II solo/rip.
ISMN M-2002-1200-6
PC 3-12

viola solo/rip.
ISMN M-2002-1201-3
PC 3-13

cello/double bass solo/rip.
ISMN M-2002-1202-0
PC 3-14

harpsichord
ISMN M-2002-1203-7
PC 3-15

No. 2 G minor
study score
ISMN M-2002-0306-6
ETP 362

separate parts:
violin I solo/rip.
ISMN M-2002-1204-4
PC 4-11

violin II solo/rip.
ISMN M-2002-1205-1
PC 4-12

viola solo/rip.
ISMN M-2002-1206-8
PC 4-13

cello/double bass solo/rip.
ISMN M-2002-1207-5
PC 4-14

harpsichord
ISMN M-2002-1208-2
PC 4-15

No. 3 E minor
study score
ISMN M-2002-0307-3
ETP 363

separate parts:
violin I solo/rip.
ISMN M-2002-1209-9
PC 5-11

violin II solo/rip.
ISMN M-2002-1210-5
PC 5-12

viola solo/rip.
ISMN M-2002-1211-2
PC 5-13

cello/double bass solo/rip.
ISMN M-2002-1212-9
PC 5-14

harpsichord
ISMN M-2002-1213-6
PC 5-15

No. 4 D minor
study score
ISMN M-2002-0308-0
ETP 364

separate parts:
violin I solo/rip.
ISMN M-2002-1272-3
PC 18-11

violin II solo/rip.
ISMN M-2002-1273-0
PC 18-12

viola solo/rip.
ISMN M-2002-1274-7
PC 18-13

cello/double bass solo/rip.
ISMN M-2002-1275-4
PC 18-14

harpsichord
ISMN M-2002-1276-1
PC 18-15

No. 5 B♭ major
study score
ISMN M-2002-0309-7
ETP 365

separate parts:
violin I solo/rip.
ISMN M-2002-1389-8
PC 45-11

violin II solo/rip.
ISMN M-2002-1390-4
PC 45-12

viola solo/rip.
ISMN M-2002-1391-1
PC 45-13

cello/double bass
ISMN M-2002-1392-8
PC 45-14

harpsichord
ISMN M-2002-1393-5
PC 45-15

No. 6 E minor
study score
ISMN M-2002-0310-3
ETP 366

separate parts:
violin I solo/rip.
ISMN M-2002-1394-2
PC 46-11

violin II solo/rip.
ISMN M-2002-1395-9
PC 46-12

viola
ISMN M-2002-1396-6
PC 46-13

cello/double bass solo/rip.
ISMN M-2002-1397-3
PC 46-14

harpsichord
ISMN M-2002-1398-0
PC 46-15

Gershwin, George

(1898-1937)

n American in Paris
ampbell-Watson)
BN 3-7957-6212-X   ISMN M-2002-1119-1
P 1398

oncerto in F
piano and orchestra
ampbell-Watson)
BN 3-7957-6222-7   ISMN M-2002-1161-0
P 1819

hapsody in Blue
piano and orchestra
BN 3-7957-6160-3   ISMN M-2002-1176-4
P 8012

Glazunov, Alexander

(1865-1936)

oncerto A minor
violin and orchestra, op. 82
BN 3-7957-6175-1   ISMN M-2002-0653-1
P 752

Glinka, Mikhail Ivanovich

(1804-1857)

amarinskaya
ntasy on two Russian Folk Songs
MN M-2002-0729-3
P 834

Life for the Tsar
as Leben für den Zaren) – Overture
BN 3-7957-7102-1   ISMN M-2002-0557-2
P 638

uslan and Lyudmila
erture to the Opera
BN 3-7957-6819-5   ISMN M-2002-0558-9
P 639   (L)

Gluck, Christoph Willibald von

(1714-1787)

higénie en Tauride
agedy in four acts
bert)
MN M-2002-0783-5
P 917

Alceste
Overture to the Opera
ISBN 3-7957-6911-6   ISMN M-2002-0937-2
ETP 1102

Iphigenia in Aulis
Overture to the Opera
ISMN M-2002-0585-5
ETP 676

Orfeo ed Euridice
Overture to the Opera
ISMN M-2002-0596-1
ETP 691

Gounod, Charles
(1818-1893)

Faust (Margarethe)
Ballet Music from the Opera (Hopkins)
ISBN 3-7957-6674-5   ISMN M-2002-1101-6
ETP 1380

Greene, Maurice
(c. 1695-1755)

Overture No. 5 D major
study score
ISMN M-2002-0962-4
ETP 1132

separate parts:
violin I
EOS 1132-11
violin II
EOS 1132-12
viola
EOS 1132-13
flute
EOS 1132-23
oboe I
EOS 1132-24
oboe II
EOS 1132-25
bassoon/basso
EOS 1132-28
basso continuo
EOS 1132-06

Overture No. 6 E♭ major
(Platt)
study score
ISMN M-2002-0963-1
ETP 1133
separate parts:
violin I
EOS 1133-11
violin II
EOS 1133-12
viola
EOS 1133-13

---

cello/bass/bassoon
EOS 1133-16
oboe I
EOS 1133-24
oboe II
EOS 1133-25
basso continuo
EOS 1133-06

Grieg, Edvard
(1843-1907)

Peer Gynt Suites Nos. 1 and 2
op. 46 / op. 55
ISBN 3-7957-6109-3   ISMN M-2002-1056-9
ETP 1318

Holberg Suite
Suite for strings, op. 40
ISMN M-2002-0765-1
ETP 897

Sigurd Jorsalfar
3 orchestral pieces from the Incidental Music,
op. 56 (Horton)
ISBN 3-7957-6950-7   ISMN M-2002-1097-2
ETP 1372

2 Elegiac Melodies
op. 34 (Horton)
ISBN 3-7957-6833-0   ISMN M-2002-1098-9
ETP 1373

Piano Concerto A minor, op. 16
ISBN 3-7957-6289-8   ISMN M-2002-0628-9
ETP 726

String Quartet G minor, op. 27
ISBN 3-7957-6285-5   ISMN M-2002-0253-3
ETP 276

Handel, George Frideric
(1685-1759)

Choral and Vocal Works

The Messiah / Der Messias
ISBN 3-7957-6305-3   ISMN M-2002-0805-4
ETP 956

Dixit Dominus
ISBN 3-7957-6948-5   ISMN M-2002-1146-7
ETP 1708

Te Deum D major
"Dettingen Te Deum" (Walker)
ISBN 3-7957-6168-9   ISMN M-2002-0796-5
ETP 945

Cornation Anthems

Zadok the Priest, HWV 258
ISMN M-2002-1140-5
ETP 1701

Let thy hand be strengthened,
HWV 259
ISMN M-2002-1141-2
ETP 1702

The King shall rejoice, HWV 260
ISBN 3-7957-6983-3   ISMN M-2002-1142-9
ETP 1703

My heart is inditing, HWV 261
ISMN M-2002-1143-6
ETP 1704

Orchestral Works

The Musick for the Royal Fireworks / Feuerwerksmusik
(Fiske)
study score
ISBN 3-7957-6645-1   ISMN M-2002-1050-7
ETP 1307
wind band parts
(3 oboes, 2 bassoons, 3 horns in C,
trumpet in C, timpani)
ISMN M-2002-1477-2
PC 61-10
separate parts:
horn I
EOS 1307-19
horn II
EOS 1307-20
horn III
EOS 1307-21
trumpet I
EOS 1307-22
trumpet II
EOS 1307-23
trumpet III
EOS 1307-24
timpani
EOS 1307-25
violin I/oboe I
ISMN M-2002-1479-6
PC 61-12
violin II/oboe II
ISMN M-2002-1480-2
PC 61-13
oboe III/viola
EOS 1307-17
viola
ISMN M-2002-1481-9
PC 61-14
cello/bassoon I
ISMN M-2002-1482-6
PC 61-15
double bass/bassoon II
ISMN M-2002-1483-3
PC 61-16
cello/double bass/bassoon
EOS 1307-15
bassoon II
EOS 1307-18
harpsichord
ISMN M-2002-1478-9
PC 61-11

The Water Music / Wassermusik
(Fiske)
study score
ISBN 3-7957-6786-5   ISMN M-2002-1051-4
ETP 1308
separate parts:
flute
ISMN M-2002-1484-0
PC 62-11
oboe I
ISMN M-2002-1485-7
PC 62-12
oboe II
ISMN M-2002-1486-4
PC 62-13
bassoon
ISMN M-2002-1487-1
PC 62-14
horn I
ISMN M-2002-1488-8
PC 62-15
horn II
ISMN M-2002-1489-5
PC 62-16
trumpet I
ISMN M-2002-1490-1
PC 62-17
trumpet II
ISMN M-2002-1491-8
PC 62-18
violin I
ISMN M-2002-1492-5
PC 62-19
violin II
ISMN M-2002-1493-2
PC 62-20
viola
ISMN M-2002-1494-9
PC 62-21
basso
ISMN M-2002-1495-6
PC 62-22
harpsichord
ISMN M-2002-1496-3
PC 62-23
basso continuo (harpsichord)
ISMN M-2002-2315-6
EOS 1308-65

Chamber Music

Trio Sonata, op. 2/1
for flute, violin and basso continuo (Lam)
ISMN M-2002-1089-7
ETP 1364

Trio Sonata, op. 2/2
for flute, violin and basso continuo (Lam)
ISMN M-2002-1090-3
ETP 1365

Trio Sonata, op. 2/3
Dresden
for 2 violins and basso continuo (Lam)
ISMN M-2002-1091-0
ETP 1366

Concertos

Concerto grosso C major
from "Alexander's Feast" /
"Das Alexanderfest" (Schroeder)
study score
ISBN 3-7957-6241-3   ISMN M-2002-0321-9
ETP 383
separate parts:
violin I solo/rip.
ISMN M-2002-1643-1
PC 90-01
violin II solo
ISMN M-2002-1644-8
PC 90-02
oboe I
ISMN M-2002-1645-5
PC 90-11
oboe II
ISMN M-2002-1646-2
PC 90-12
violin II rip.
ISMN M-2002-1647-9
PC 90-14
viola
ISMN M-2002-1648-6
PC 90-15
harpsichord
ISMN M-2002-1650-9
PC 90-17

Concerti grossi, op. 3
„Oboe Concertos" (Sadie)
No. 1 B♭ major
study score
ISMN M-2002-0315-8
ETP 377
wind band parts
(2 flutes, 2 oboes, 2 bassoons)
ISMN M-2002-1509-0
PC 66-10
separate parts:
harpsichord
ISMN M-2002-1510-6
PC 66-11
violin I
ISMN M-2002-1511-3
PC 66-12
violin II
ISMN M-2002-1512-0
PC 66-13
viola
ISMN M-2002-1513-7
PC 66-14
cello/double bass
ISMN M-2002-1514-4
PC 66-15

, 2 B♭ major
dy score
MN M-2002-0316-5
378

o parts:
in I
MN M-2002-1515-1
67-01
in II
MN M-2002-1516-8
67-02
o I
MN M-2002-1517-5
67-03
o II
MN M-2002-1518-2
67-04
nd band parts (2 oboes, bassoon)
MN M-2002-1519-9
67-10
arate parts:
in I rip.
MN M-2002-1521-2
67-12
in II rip.
MN M-2002-1522-9
67-13
a
MN M-2002-1523-6
67-14
si
MN M-2002-1524-3
67-15
psichord
MN M-2002-1520-5
67-11

, 3 G major
dy score
MN M-2002-0317-2
379

o parts:
e/oboe
MN M-2002-1525-0
68-01
in
MN M-2002-1526-7
68-02
arate parts:
in I
MN M-2002-1527-4
68-11
in II
MN M-2002-1528-1
68-12
a
MN M-2002-1529-8
68-13
si
MN M-2002-1530-4
68-14
psichord
MN M-2002-1531-1
58-15

No. 4 F major
(Hudson/Redlich)
study score
ISMN M-2002-0313-4
ETP 374
solo parts:
oboe I
ISMN M-2002-1411-6
PC 50-11
oboe II
ISMN M-2002-1412-3
PC 50-12
separate parts:
violin I
ISMN M-2002-1413-0
PC 50-13
violin II
ISMN M-2002-1414-7
PC 50-14
viola
ISMN M-2002-1415-4
PC 50-15
cello/basso continuo
ISMN M-2002-1416-1
PC 50-16
harpsichord
ISMN M-2002-1417-8
PC 50-17
solo parts:
oboe I
EOS 374-14
oboe II
EOS 374-15
separate parts:
violin I
EOS 374-11
violin II
EOS 374-12
viola
EOS 374-13
basso
EOS 374-16
basso continuo
EOS 374-17

No. 4a F major
study score
ISMN M-2002-0318-9
ETP 380
solo parts:
oboe I
ISMN M-2002-1532-8
PC 69-11
oboe II
ISMN M-2002-1533-5
PC 69-12
separate parts:
violin I
ISMN M-2002-1534-2
PC 69-13
violin II
ISMN M-2002-1535-9
PC 69-14

viola
ISMN M-2002-1536-6
PC 69-15
cello/double bass
ISMN M-2002-1537-3
PC 69-16
harpsichord
ISMN M-2002-1538-0
PC 69-17

No. 5 D minor
study score
ISMN M-2002-0319-6
ETP 381
solo parts:
oboe I
ISMN M-2002-1539-7
PC 70-11
oboe II
ISMN M-2002-1540-3
PC 70-12
separate parts:
violin I
ISMN M-2002-1541-0
PC 70-13
violin II
ISMN M-2002-1542-7
PC 70-14
viola
ISMN M-2002-1543-4
PC 70-15
cello/double bass/bassoon
ISMN M-2002-1544-1
PC 70-16
harpsichord
ISMN M-2002-1545-8
PC 70-17

No. 6 D major
study score
ISMN M-2002-0320-2
ETP 382
solo parts:
oboe I
ISMN M-2002-1546-5
PC 71-11
oboe II
ISMN M-2002-1547-2
PC 71-12
separate parts:
violin I
ISMN M-2002-1548-9
PC 71-13
violin II
ISMN M-2002-1549-6
PC 71-14
viola
ISMN M-2002-1550-2
PC 71-15
cello/double bass
ISMN M-2002-1551-9
PC 71-16
harpsichord
ISMN M-2002-1552-6
PC 71-17

Concerti grossi, op. 6
(1739) (Nyman)

No. 1 G major
ISBN 3-7957-6813-6   ISMN M-2002-0240-3
ETP 263

No. 2 F major
ISMN M-2002-0241-0
ETP 264

No. 3 E minor
ISMN M-2002-0242-7
ETP 265

No. 4 A minor
ISMN M-2002-0243-4
ETP 266

No. 5 D major
ISMN M-2002-0244-1
ETP 267

No. 6 G minor
ISBN 3-7957-6363-0   ISMN M-2002-0245-8
ETP 268

No. 7 B♭ major
ISMN M-2002-0246-5
ETP 269

No. 8 C minor
ISBN 3-7957-6615-X   ISMN M-2002-0247-2
ETP 270

No. 9 F major
ISMN M-2002-0248-9
ETP 271

No. 10 D minor
ISMN M-2002-0249-6
ETP 272

No. 11 A major
ISMN M-2002-0250-2
ETP 273

No. 12 B minor
ISMN M-2002-0251-9
ETP 274

Organ Concertos, op. 4
(Williams)

No. 1 G minor
ISBN 3-7957-6978-7   ISMN M-2002-1148-1
ETP 1801

No. 2 B♭ major
ISMN M-2002-1149-8
ETP 1802

No. 3 G minor
ISMN M-2002-1150-4
ETP 1803

No. 4 F major
ISMN M-2002-1151-1
ETP 1804

No. 5 F major
ISMN M-2002-1152-8
ETP 1805

No. 6 B♭ major
"Harp Concerto" / "Harfenkonzert"

study score
ISMN M-2002-1153-5
ETP 1806

score
ISMN M-001-04555-1
ED 3831

organ score (= harp)
ISMN M-001-04507-0
ED 3806

separate parts:
flute (treble recorder) I
ISMN M-001-04556-8
ED 3831-11

flute (treble recorder) II
ISMN M-001-04557-5
ED 3831-12

violin I
ISMN M-001-04558-2
ED 3831-13

violin II
ISMN M-001-04559-9
ED 3831-14

viola
ISMN M-001-04560-5
ED 3831-15

bassi
ISMN M-001-04561-2
ED 3831-16

Organ Concerti, op. 7

No. 1 B♭ major
ISMN M-2002-1038-5
ETP 1291

No. 2 A major
ISMN M-2002-1039-2
ETP 1292

No. 3 B♭ major
ISMN M-2002-1040-8
ETP 1293

No. 4 D minor
ISMN M-2002-1041-5
ETP 1294

No. 5 G minor
ISMN M-2002-1042-2
ETP 1295

No. 6 B♭ major
ISMN M-2002-1043-9
ETP 1296

Hasse,
Johann Adolf
(1699-1783)

Concerto D major
for flute, strings and basso continuo
ISMN M-2002-0968-6
ETP 1203

Haydn,
Joseph
(1732-1809)

Choral and Vocal Works

Die Schöpfung
(The Creation), Hob.XXI:2
ISBN 3-7957-6191-3   ISMN M-2002-0804-7
ETP 955

Die Jahreszeiten
(The Seasons) Hob.XXI:3
ISBN 3-7957-6317-7   ISMN M-2002-0833-7
ETP 987

Missa in Angustiis D minor
"Nelson Mass" (Landon)
ISBN 3-7957-6838-1   ISMN M-2002-0839-9
ETP 995   (L)

Missa Sancti Nicolai G major
Hob. XXII:6 (Landon)
ISBN 3-7957-6892-6   ISMN M-2002-0935-8
ETP 1099

Orchestral Works

Symphonies
No. 6 D major
"Le Matin", Hob. I:6 (Landon)
ISBN 3-7957-6916-7   ISMN M-2002-0458-2
ETP 536

No. 7 C major
"Le Midi", Hob. I:7 (Praetorius)
ISBN 3-7957-6993-0   ISMN M-2002-0440-7
ETP 513

No. 8 G major
"Le Soir" / „La Tempesta", Hob. I:8
(Landon)
ISMN M-2002-0442-1
ETP 515

No. 13 D major
(1763), Hob. I:13 (Landon)
ISMN M-2002-0483-4
ETP 563

No. 21 A major
(1764), Hob. I:21 (Landon)
ISMN M-2002-0481-0
ETP 561

No. 22 E♭ major
"Der Philosoph", Hob. I:22 (Hochkofler)
ISMN M-2002-0467-4
ETP 545

No. 26 D minor
"Lamentatione", Hob. I:26 (Landon)
ISBN 3-7957-6975-2   ISMN M-2002-0471-1
ETP 550

No. 29 E major
(1765), Hob. I:29 (Landon)
ISMN M-2002-0482-7
ETP 562

. 31 D major
it dem Hornsignal - Auf dem Anstand"
b. I:31 (Praetorius)
3N 3-7957-6967-1   ISMN M-2002-0439-1
P 512

. 34 D major
b. I:34 (Beechey)
vIN M-2002-0504-6
P 584

. 35 B♭ major
'67), Hob. I:35 (Landon)
vIN M-2002-0484-1
P 564

. 39 G minor
b. I:39 (Landon)
vIN M-2002-0472-8
P 551

. 44 E minor
auersinfonie", Hob. I:44 (Landon)
3N 3-7957-6740-7   ISMN M-2002-0466-7
P 544

. 45 F minor
arewell" / "Abschieds-Sinfonie"Hob. I: 45
3N 3-7957-6642-7   ISMN M-2002-0418-6
P 486

. 46 B major
'72), Hob. I:46 (Beechey)
3N 3-7957-6880-2   ISMN M-2002-0451-3
P 528

. 48 C major
laria Theresia", Hob. I:48 (Praetorius)
vIN M-2002-0444-5
P 517

. 49 F minor
a Passione", Hob. I:49 (Landon)
3N 3-7957-6830-6   ISMN M-2002-0457-5
P 535

. 50 C major
b. I:50 (Beechey)
vIN M-2002-0508-4
P 588

. 51 B♭ major
b. I:51 (Beechey)
vIN M-2002-0505-3
P 585

. 52 C minor
b. I:52 (Newstone)
vIN M-2002-0485-8
P 565

. 53 D major
Impériale" mit alternierendem Finale
b. I:53 (Landon)
3N 3-7957-6739-3   ISMN M-2002-0459-9
P 537

. 54 G major
'74), Hob. I:54 (Beechey)
vIN M-2002-0514-5
P 594

No. 55 E♭ major
"The Schoolmaster" / "Der Schulmeister"
Hob. I:55 (Landon)
ISMN M-2002-0445-2
ETP 518

No. 57 D major
(1774), Hob. I:57 (Newstone)
ISMN M-2002-0491-9
ETP 571

No. 59 A major
"Fire" / "Feuer", Hob. I:59 (Beechey)
ISMN M-2002-0517-6
ETP 597

No. 60 C major
"Il Distratto", Hob. I: 60 (Beechey)
ISBN 3-7957-6908-6   ISMN M-2002-0503-9
ETP 583

No. 63 C major
"La Roxelane" – 2 Versions, Hob. I:63
ISMN M-2002-0477-3
ETP 557

No. 69 C major
"Laudon", Hob. I:69 (Beechey)
ISMN M-2002-0509-1
ETP 589

No. 70 D major
Hob. I:70 (Landon)
ISMN M-2002-0479-7
ETP 559

No. 73 D major
"La Chasse", Hob. I:73 (Praetorius)
ISMN M-2002-0438-4
ETP 511

No. 80 D minor
(1784), Hob. I:80 (Newstone)
ISMN M-2002-0492-6
ETP 572

"Paris" Symphonies
No. 82 C major,
"L'Ours", Hob. I:82 (Praetorius)
ISBN 3-7957-6766-0   ISMN M-2002-0420-9
ETP 488

No. 83 G minor
"La Poule", Hob. I:83 (Redlich)
ISBN 3-7957-6895-0   ISMN M-2002-0452-0
ETP 530

No. 84 E♭ major
Hob. I:84 (Landon)
ISMN M-2002-0456-8
ETP 534

No. 85 B♭ major,
"La Reine", Hob. I:85 (Praetorius)
ISBN 3-7957-6336-3   ISMN M-2002-0369-1
ETP 432

No. 86 D major
Hob. I:86 (Praetorius)
ISBN 3-7957-6324-X   ISMN M-2002-0416-2
ETP 484

No. 87 A major
Hob. I:87 (Landon)
ISMN M-2002-0455-1
ETP 533

No. 88 G major
Hob. I:88 (Praetorius)
ISMN M-2002-0419-3
ETP 487

No. 89 F major
(1787), Hob. I:89 (Landon)
ISBN 3-7957-6300-2   ISMN M-2002-0478-0
ETP 558

No. 90 C major
(1788), Hob. I:90 (Päuler)
ISMN M-2002-0501-5
ETP 581

No. 91 E♭ major
(1788), Hob. I:91 (Päuler)
ISMN M-2002-0502-2
ETP 582

No. 92 G major
"Oxford", Hob. I:92 (Landon)
ISMN M-2002-0373-8
ETP 436

"London" Symphonies
(Newstone)
No. 93 D major
"Glocken", Hob. I:93
ISMN M-2002-0402-5
ETP 468

No. 94 G major
"Surprise" / "Paukenschlag", Hob. I:94
ISBN 3-7957-6702-4   ISMN M-2002-0372-1
ETP 435

No. 95 C minor
Hob. I:95
ISBN 3-7957-6862-4   ISMN M-2002-0412-4
ETP 480

No. 96 D major
"Mirakel", Hob. I:96
ISMN M-2002-0413-1
ETP 481

No. 97 C major
Hob. I:97 (Praetorius)
ISBN 3-7957-6620-6   ISMN M-2002-0415-5
ETP 483

No. 98 B♭ major
Hob. I:98 (Landon)
ISBN 3-7957-6730-X   ISMN M-2002-0417-9
ETP 485

No. 99 E♭ major
Hob. I:99
ISBN 3-7957-6866-7   ISMN M-2002-0368-4
ETP 431

No. 100 G major
"Military", Hob. I:100
study score
ISMN M-2002-0371-4
ETP 434

set of string parts
ISBN 3-7957-6765-2   ISMN M-2002-1911-1
EOS 434-50

set of wind parts
ISBN 3-7957-6764-4   ISMN M-2002-1912-8
EOS 434-60

separate parts:
violin I
ISBN 3-7957-6780-6   ISMN M-2002-1894-7
EOS 434-11

violin II
ISBN 3-7957-6781-4   ISMN M-2002-1895-4
EOS 434-12

viola
ISBN 3-7957-6782-2   ISMN M-2002-1896-1
EOS 434-13

cello
ISBN 3-7957-6783-0   ISMN M-2002-1897-8
EOS 434-14

double bass
ISBN 3-7957-6784-9   ISMN M-2002-1898-5
EOS 434-15

No. 101 D major
"The Clock" / "Die Uhr", Hob. I:101
ISBN 3-7957-6785-7   ISMN M-2002-0376-9
ETP 439

No. 102 B♭ major
Hob. I:102
ISBN 3-7957-6861-6   ISMN M-2002-0375-2
ETP 438

No. 103 E♭ major
"Drum Roll" / "Paukenwirbel", Hob. I:103
ISBN 3-7957-6940-X   ISMN M-2002-0403-2
ETP 469

No. 104 D major
"Salomon", Hob. I:104
study score
ISBN 3-7957-6698-2   ISMN M-2002-0346-2
ETP 409
wind band parts
ISMN M-2002-1834-3
EOS 409-60
set of string parts
ISMN M-2002-1833-6
EOS 409-50

separate parts:
violin I
ISMN M-2002-1828-2
EOS 409-11
violin II
ISMN M-2002-1829-9
EOS 409-12
viola
ISMN M-2002-1830-5
EOS 409-13
cello
ISMN M-2002-1831-2
EOS 409-14
double bass
ISMN M-2002-1832-9
EOS 409-15

L'Isola disabitata
Overture (1779), Hob. Ia:13 (Landon)
ISMN M-2002-0955-6
ETP 1124

Die Feuersbrunst
Overture to "Opéra comique vom abgebrannten
Haus", Hob. XXIXb: A (Landon)
ISMN M-2002-0958-7
ETP 1128   (L)

Concertos

Sinfonia concertante B♭ major
for oboe, bassoon, violin, violoncello and
orchestra, Hob. I:105 (Landon)
ISBN 3-7957-6299-5   ISMN M-2002-0691-3
ETP 790

Violin Concerto C major
Hob. VIIa:1 (Landon)
ISBN 3-7957-6792-X   ISMN M-2002-0967-9
ETP 1202

Violin Concerto G major
Hob. VIIa:4 (Landon)
ISBN 3-7957-6185-9   ISMN M-2002-0988-4
ETP 1228

Cello Concerto D major
op. 101 (1783), Hob. VIIb:2 (Schönzeler)
ISBN 3-7957-6810-1   ISMN M-2002-0670-8
ETP 769

Horn Concerto D major
(1762), Hob. VIId:3 (Landon)
ISBN 3-7957-7146-3   ISMN M-2002-0991-4
ETP 1232

Trumpet Concerto Eb major
Hob. VIIe:1 (Redlich)
ISBN 3-7957-6790-3   ISMN M-2002-0699-9
ETP 798

Concerto D major
for harpsichord (piano) and orchestra,
Hob. XVIII:11 (Soldan)
ISBN 3-7957-6851-9   ISMN M-2002-0692-0
ETP 791

Chamber Music

String Quartets, op. 1
No. 1 B♭ major, Hob. III:1
ISMN M-2002-0176-5
ETP 170

No. 2 E♭ major, Hob. III:2
ISMN M-2002-0177-2
ETP 171

No. 4 G major, Hob. III:4
ISBN 3-7957-6608-7   ISMN M-2002-0155-0
ETP 149

No. 5 B♭ major, Hob. III:5
ISMN M-2002-0179-6
ETP 173

No. 6 C major, Hob. III:6
ISMN M-2002-0180-2
ETP 174

String Quartets, op. 2
(1764) (Altmann)
No. 1 A major, Hob. III:7
ISMN M-2002-0181-9
ETP 175

No. 2 E major, Hob. III: 8
ISMN M-2002-0182-6
ETP 176

No. 3 E♭ major, Hob. III:9
ISBN 3-7957-7114-5   ISMN M-2002-0183-3
ETP 177

No. 4 F major, Hob. III: 10
ISMN M-2002-0184-0
ETP 178

No. 5 D major, Hob. III:11
ISMN M-2002-0185-7
ETP 179

No. 6 B♭ major, Hob. III: 12
ISBN 3-7957-7129-3   ISMN M-2002-0186-4
ETP 180

String Quartets, op. 3
(1767) (Altmann)
No. 1 E major, Hob. III: 13
ISMN M-2002-0187-1
ETP 181

No. 2 C major, Hob. III: 14
ISMN M-2002-0188-8
ETP 182

No. 3 G major, Hob. III:15
Dudelsack-Menuett
ISMN M-2002-0189-5
ETP 183

No. 4 B♭ major, Hob. III:16
ISMN M-2002-0190-1
ETP 184

No. 5 F major, Hob. III: 17
"Serenade"
ISMN M-2002-0156-7
ETP 150

No. 6 A major, Hob. III:18
ISMN M-2002-0191-8
ETP 185

String Quartets, op. 9
(1769) (Altmann)
No. 1 C major, Hob. III:19
ISMN M-2002-0109-3
ETP 89

No. 2 E♭ major, Hob. III:20
ISMN M-2002-0157-4
ETP 151

No. 3 G major, Hob. III:21
ISMN M-2002-0192-5
ETP 186

No. 4 D minor, Hob. III:22
ISMN M-2002-0115-4
ETP 95

. 5 B♭ major, Hob. III:23
MN M-2002-0193-2
P 187

. 6 A major, Hob. III:24
MN M-2002-0194-9
Ⴢ 188

ːring Quartets, op. 17
ϸ71) (Altmann)
Ͻ. 1 E major, Hob. III: 25
MN M-2002-0130-7
Ⴥ 111

. 2 F major, Hob. III:26
MN M-2002-0148-2
Ⴥ 142

). 4 C minor, Hob. III: 28
MN M-2002-0158-1
Ⴢ 152

). 6 D major, Hob. III:30
MN M-2002-0110-9
Ⴥ 90

ːun Quartets" / ːonnen-Quartette", op. 20
ϸ72) (Altmann)
Ͻ. 1 E♭ major, Hob. III:31
ℬN 3-7957-7115-3   ISMN M-2002-0169-7
Ⴥ 163

). 2 C major, Hob. III: 32
ℬN 3-7957-6999-X   ISMN M-2002-0127-7
Ⴥ 108

. 3 G minor, Hob. III: 33
MN M-2002-0170-3
Ⴥ 164

. 4 D major, Hob. III: 34
MN M-2002-0113-0
Ⴥ 93

). 6 A major, Hob. III: 36
MN M-2002-0084-3
Ⴥ 64

ːRussian Quartets" / ːRussische Quartette", op. 33
ϸtmann)
Ͻ. 1 B minor, Hob. III: 37
MN M-2002-0171-0
Ⴥ 165

). 2 E♭ major, Hob. III: 38
ℬN 3-7957-6873-X   ISMN M-2002-0073-7
Ⴥ 52

). 3 C major, Hob. III: 39
ːhe Bird" / "Vogel"
MN M-2002-0074-4
Ⴥ 53

). 4 B♭ major, Hob. III: 40
MN M-2002-0172-7
Ⴥ 166

). 5 G major, Hob. III: 41
MN M-2002-0159-8
Ⴥ 153

No. 6 D major, Hob. III: 42
ISMN M-2002-0195-6
ETP 189

No. 6 D minor, op. 42, Hob. III:43
ISMN M-2002-0160-4
ETP 154

"Prussian Quartets" / "Preußische Quartette", op. 50
(1787) (Altmann)
No. 1 B♭ major, Hob. III: 44
ISMN M-2002-0173-4
ETP 167

No. 2 C major, Hob. III:45
ISMN M-2002-0174-1
ETP 168

No. 3 E♭ major, Hob. III:46
ISMN M-2002-0175-8
ETP 169

No. 4 F minor, Hob. III: 47
ISMN M-2002-0131-4
ETP 112

No. 5 F major, Hob. III: 48
"The Dream" / "Der Traum"
ISMN M-2002-0161-1
ETP 155

No. 6 D major, Hob. III:49
"Frog" / "Frosch"
ISMN M-2002-0162-8
ETP 156

Die sieben Worte Jesu Christi
(The seven words of Jesus Christ)
7 String Quartets, op. 51, Hob. III: 50-56
ISBN 3-7957-6693-1   ISMN M-2002-0168-0
ETP 162

"Tost-Quartette I"
op. 54/op. 55 (1788) (Altmann)
No. 1 C major, op. 54/1, Hob. III: 57
ISBN 3-7957-6969-8   ISMN M-2002-0086-7
ETP 66

No. 2 G major, op. 54/2 Hob. III:58
ISBN 3-7957-6897-7   ISMN M-2002-0075-1
ETP 54

No. 3 E major, op. 54/3, Hob. III:59
ISMN M-2002-0132-1
ETP 113

No. 4 A major, op. 55/1, Hob. III: 60
ISMN M-2002-0116-1
ETP 96

No. 5 F minor, op. 55/2, Hob. III: 61
"Razor" / "Rasiermesser"
ISMN M-2002-0196-3
ETP 190

No. 6 B♭ major, op. 55/3, Hob. III: 62
ISMN M-2002-0149-9
ETP 143

"Tost-Quartette II"
op. 64 (1790) (Altmann)
No. 1 D major, Hob. III: 67
"Lerchen"
ISBN 3-7957-6834-9   ISMN M-2002-0076-8
ETP 55

No. 2 E♭ major, Hob. III:64
ISMN M-2002-0112-3
ETP 92

No. 3 C major, Hob. III:65
ISBN 3-7957-7141-2   ISMN M-2002-0150-5
ETP 144

No. 4 G major, Hob. III:66
ISMN M-2002-0111-6
ETP 91

No. 5 B♭ major, Hob. III:67
ISMN M-2002-0085-0
ETP 65

No. 6 B minor, Hob. III:68
ISMN M-2002-0128-4
ETP 109

"Apponyi-Quartette"
op. 71/ op. 74 (1793) (Altmann)
No. 1 B♭ majeur
op. 71/1, Hob. III: 69
ISBN 3-7957-6759-8   ISMN M-2002-0129-1
ETP 110

No. 2 D major
op. 71/2, Hob. III: 70
ISBN 3-7957-6346-0   ISMN M-2002-0151-2
ETP 145

No. 3 E♭ major
op. 71/3, Hob. III:71
ISMN M-2002-0154-3
ETP 148

No. 4 C major
op. 74/1, Hob. III: 72
ISMN M-2002-0152-9
ETP 146

No. 5 F major
op. 74/2, Hob. III: 73
ISMN M-2002-0153-6
ETP 147

No. 6 G minor
"Reiter", op. 74/3, Hob. III: 74
ISBN 3-7957-6840-3   ISMN M-2002-0079-9
ETP 58

"Erdödy-Quartette"
op. 76 (1799) (Altmann)
No. 1 G major, Hob. III: 75
ISBN 3-7957-6742-3   ISMN M-2002-0089-8
ETP 69

No. 2 D minor, Hob. III: 76
"Quinten"
ISBN 3-7957-6850-0   ISMN M-2002-0033-1
ETP 10

No. 3 C major, Hob. III:77
"Emperor" / "Kaiserquartett" (Döge)
ISBN 3-7957-6110-7   ISMN M-2002-0027-0
ETP 3

No. 4 B♭ major, Hob. III: 78
"L'Aurore"
ISBN 3-7957-6758-X   ISMN M-2002-0077-5
ETP 56

No. 5 D major, Hob. III: 79
"Celebrated Largo"
ISBN 3-7957-6998-1   ISMN M-2002-0078-2
ETP 57

No. 6 E♭ major, Hob. III:80
ISBN 3-7957-6914-0   ISMN M-2002-0197-0
ETP 191

String Quartet G major
Hob. III: 81
„Komplimentier", op. 77/1 (Altmann)
ISBN 3-7957-6754-7   ISMN M-2002-0082-9
ETP 61

String Quartet F major
op. 77/2
Hob. III: 82 (Altmann)
ISMN M-2002-0299-1
ETP 355

String Quartet B♭ major,op. 103
(Unfinished) Hob. III:83
(1803) (Altmann)
ISMN M-2002-0300-4
ETP 356

Piano Trio G major
with Rondo all'Ongarese, Hob. XV: 25
ISBN 3-7957-6980-9   ISMN M-2002-0238-0
ETP 259

Heinichen, Johann David
(1683-1729)

Concerto in D major
for flute, oboe, violin, cello, theorbo, strings and
basso continuo (Haußwald)
study score
ISMN M-2002-0331-8
ETP 393
solo parts:
flute
ISMN M-2002-1708-7
PC 101-01
oboe
ISMN M-2002-1709-4
PC 101-02
violin
ISMN M-2002-1710-0
PC 101-03
theorbo
ISMN M-2002-1711-7
PC 101-04

separate parts:
violin I/II
ISMN M-2002-1712-4
PC 101-11
viola
ISMN M-2002-1713-1
PC 101-12
cello solo/rip./double bass
ISMN M-2002-1714-8
PC 101-13
harpsichord
ISMN M-2002-1715-5
PC 101-14

Hindemith, Paul
(1895-1963)

Cardillac
Opera in 3 Acts (original version), op. 39
(1925-26) (Wolff)
ISMN M-2002-1177-1
ETP 8013   (L)

Klaviermusik mit Orchester
(Klavier: linke Hand / piano: left hand)
op. 29 (1923)
ISMN 2002-2316-3
ETP 1899   (L) i.V. / in prep.

Konzert für Orchester
op. 38 (1925) (Schubert)
ISMN M-2002-1190-0
ETP 8036   (L)

Konzertmusik
for string orchestra and brass, op. 50
(1930) (Werner-Jensen)
ISBN 3-7957-6293-6   ISMN M-2002-2050-6
ETP 1460   (L)

Symphonie "Mathis der Maler"
(1934) (Kemp)
ISBN 3-7957-6173-5   ISMN M-2002-0493-3
ETP 573

Symphonische Metamorphosen
of Themes by C.M. von Weber (1943) (Kemp)
ISBN 3-7957-6252-9   ISMN M-2002-1115-3
ETP 1394

Der Schwanendreher
Concerto after old Folksongs
for viola and small orchestra (1935-36)
ISBN 3-7957-6283-9   ISMN M-2002-1159-7
ETP 1816   (L)

Septet
for flute, oboe, clarinet, trumpet, french horn,
bass clarinet and bassoon (1948)
(Schubert)
ISMN M-2002-1126-9
ETP 1407

Holst, Gustav
(1874-1934)

Savitri, op. 25
Opera di camera
ISBN 3-7957-6917-5   ISMN M-2002-0933-4
ETP 1097

A Choral Fantasia, op. 51
ISMN M-2002-0934-1
ETP 1098

The Planets, op. 32
Suite (Holst/Matthews)
ISBN 3-7957-6877-2   ISMN M-2002-1172-6
ETP 8007

Honegger, Arthur
(1892-1955)

Pacific 231
Symphonic Movement (Schneider)
ISBN 3-7957-6164-6   ISMN M-2002-1118-4
ETP 1397

Symphony No. 3
"Liturgique" (Schneider)
ISBN 3-7957-6272-3   ISMN M-2002-1135-1
ETP 1518

Symphony No. 5
"di tre re" (1950) (Schneider)
ISBN 3-7957-7131-5   ISMN M-2002-1136-8
ETP 1519

Hummel, Johann Nepomuk
(1778-1837)

Concerto E major
for trumpet and orchestra (Haan)
ISBN 3-7957-6893-4   ISMN M-2002-1046-0
ETP 1299

Humperdinck, Engelbert
(1854-1921)

Hänsel und Gretel
Fairy Opera (1883)
ISBN 3-7957-6169-7   ISMN M-2002-0779-8
ETP 913   (L)

Hänsel und Gretel
Prelude to the Fairy Opera
ISBN 3-7957-6951-5   ISMN M-2002-0936-5
ETP 1101

Janáček, Leos
(1854-1928)

■fonietta
(rghauser)
N 3-7957-6818-7   ISMN M-2002-1094-1
■ 1369

Korngold, Erich Wolfgang
(1897-1957)

■nzert in D-Dur
violin and orchestra, op. 35
37-39/45)
N 3-7957-6857-8   ISMN M-2002-2314-9
■ 1898   in prep.

mphony in F♯
40 (1947-52) (Pöllmann)
N 3-7957-6214-6   ISMN M-2002-2005-6
■ 8048   (L)

Lalo, Edouard
(1823-1892)

Roi d'Ys
erture
MN M-2002-0939-6
■ 1104   (L)

mphonie espagnole
violin and orchestra, op. 21
N 3-7957-6687-7   ISMN M-2002-0630-2
■ 728   (L)

Leo, Leonardo
(1694-1744)

■nfonia G minor
roduzione dall'Oratorio:
anta Elena al Calvario" (Engländer)
MN M-2002-0460-5
P 538

■ncerto D major
cello, strings and basso continuo
:hroeder)
MN M-2002-0980-8
■ 1218

Liszt, Franz
(1811-1886)

Choral and Vocal Works

Missa choralis
study score (= vocal score)
ISBN 3-7957-6247-2   ISMN M-2002-0918-1
ETP 1076

Missa coronationalis
(Coronation Mass / Krönungsmesse)
(Sulyok)
ISMN M-2002-0792-7
ETP 941

Missa Solemnis
Graner Festmesse (Sulyok)
ISMN M-2002-0793-4
ETP 942

Requiem
(Darvas)
ISMN M-2002-0797-2
ETP 947

Via crucis
The 14 Stations of the Cross
ISMN M-2002-0924-2
ETP 1082

Orchestral Works

Dante Symphony
for Dantes Divina Commedia
for female chorus and orchestra (Sulyok)
ISBN 3-7957-6262-6   ISMN M-2002-0510-7
ETP 590

Eine Faust-Sinfonie
in 3 character-pictures
for tenor, male chorus and orchestra
ISBN 3-7957-6218-9   ISMN M-2002-0410-0
ETP 477

**Phantasie über
Ungarische Volksmelodien**
(Fantasia on Hungarian Folk Themes)
ISBN 3-7957-7124-2   ISMN M-2002-1045-3
ETP 1298

Symphonic Poems
**No. 1 Ce qu'on entend
sur la montagne**
ISMN M-2002-0384-4
ETP 447

No. 3 Les Préludes
ISBN 3-7957-6658-3   ISMN M-2002-0386-8
ETP 449

No. 4 Orpheus
ISMN M-2002-0387-5
ETP 450

No. 5 Prometheus
ISBN 3-7957-7137-4   ISMN M-2002-0388-2
ETP 451

No. 6 Mazeppa
ISMN M-2002-0389-9
ETP 452

No. 7 Festklänge
ISMN M-2002-0390-5
ETP 453

No. 8 Héröide funèbre
(Heldenklage)
ISMN M-2002-0391-2
ETP 454

No. 9 Hungaria
ISMN M-2002-0392-9
ETP 455

No. 10 Hamlet
ISMN M-2002-0393-6
ETP 456

No. 11 Die Hunnenschlacht
(The Battle of Huns)
ISMN M-2002-0394-3
ETP 457

No. 12 Die Ideale
ISMN M-2002-0395-0
ETP 458

**No. 13
Von der Wiege bis zum Grabe**
(From the Cradle to the Grave)
ISMN M-2002-0520-6
ETP 600

2 Episoden aus Lenaus 'Faust'
ISMN M-2002-1086-6
ETP 1361

Concertos

Piano Concerto No. 1 E♭ major
ISBN 3-7957-6721-0   ISMN M-2002-0612-8
ETP 710

Piano Concerto No. 2 A major
ISBN 3-7957-6808-X   ISMN M-2002-0622-7
ETP 720   (L)

Totentanz
for piano and orchestra (original version)
ISBN 3-7957-7134-X   ISMN M-2002-0624-1
ETP 722

Wanderer-Fantasie
transcribed by Franz Liszt
for piano and orchestra, op. 15, D 760
ISMN M-2002-1047-7
ETP 1300   (L)

Liadov, Anatol Konstantinovich
(1855-1914)

The Enchanted Lake
(Der verzauberte See)
A Fairy Picture for Orchestra, op. 62
ISMN M-2002-0735-4
ETP 853

Locatelli, Pietro
(1695-1764)

L'Arte del Violino
for violin and orchestra, op. 3

Concerti No. 1-4
ISBN 3-7957-6338-X   ISMN M-2002-2307-1
ETP 1883

Concerti No. 5-8
ISBN 3-7957-6339-8   ISMN M-2002-2308-8
ETP 1887

Concerti No. 9-12
ISBN 3-7957-6340-1   ISMN M-2002-2309-5
ETP 1891

Locke, Matthew
(c. 1630-1677)

Consort of Four Parts
ISMN M-2002-1082-8
ETP 1356

The Flat Consort
ISMN M-2002-1083-5
ETP 1357

Lortzing, Albert
(1801-1851)

Zar und Zimmermann
(Czar and Carpenter) Overture
ISMN M-2002-0598-5
ETP 693

Mahler, Gustav
(1860-1911)

Choral and Vocal Works

Kindertotenlieder
(Ballstaedt/Döge)
ISBN 3-7957-6129-8   ISMN M-2002-0903-7
ETP 1060   (L)

**Lieder eines
fahrenden Gesellen**
(Songs of a Wayfarer) (Schwarz)
ISBN 3-7957-6647-8   ISMN M-2002-0896-2
ETP 1053

Orchestral Works

Symphony No. 1 D major
"The Titan" (Redlich)
ISBN 3-7957-6136-0   ISMN M-2002-0490-2
ETP 570

Symphony No. 4 G major
(Redlich)
ISBN 3-7957-6204-9   ISMN M-2002-0495-7
ETP 575

Symphony No. 5 C minor
(Ratz)
ISBN 3-7957-6194-8   ISMN M-2002-0454-4
ETP 532

Symphony No. 6 A minor
(Redlich)
ISBN 3-7957-6152-2   ISMN M-2002-0506-0
ETP 586

Symphony No. 7 E minor
(Redlich)
ISBN 3-7957-6314-2   ISMN M-2002-0423-0
ETP 492

Marschner,
Heinrich
(1795-1861)

Hans Heiling
Overture to the Opera
ISMN M-2002-0553-4
ETP 633

Mendelssohn
Bartholdy, Felix
(1809-1847)

Choral and Vokal Works

Elias
Oratorio, op. 70 (Todd)
ISBN 3-7957-6135-2   ISMN M-2002-0835-1
ETP 989

Orchestral Works

Symphonies
No. 1 C minor, op. 11
ISMN M-2002-0496-4
ETP 576

No. 2 B♭ major, op. 52
"Hymn of Praise" / "Lobgesang" (Fiske)
ISBN 3-7957-6633-8   ISMN M-2002-1178-8
ETP 8014

No. 3 A minor, op. 56
"Scottish" / "Schottische" (Haken/Roddewig)
ISBN 3-7957-6858-6   ISMN M-2002-0343-1
ETP 406

No. 4 A major, op. 90
"Italian" / "Italienische" (1830-33) (Fiske)
ISBN 3-7957-6776-8   ISMN M-2002-0357-8
ETP 420

No. 5 D minor, op. 107
"Reformation" (Alberti)
ISBN 3-7957-6715-6   ISMN M-2002-0474-2
ETP 554

Ein Sommernachtstraum
5 Orchestral Pieces, op. 61/1, 5, 7, 9, 11
(A Midsummer Night's Dream) (Fiske)
ISBN 3-7957-7138-2   ISMN M-2002-0705-7
ETP 804

Ein Sommernachtstraum
Overture (Whittaker)
ISBN 3-7957-6815-2   ISMN M-2002-0533-6
ETP 613

Die Hebriden / The Hebrides
Overture, op. 26
ISBN 3-7957-6708-3   ISMN M-2002-0556-5
ETP 637

**Meeresstille und
glückliche Fahrt**
(Calm Sea and Prosperous Voyage)
Overture for Orchestra, op. 27
ISBN 3-7957-6797-0   ISMN M-2002-0567-1
ETP 653

Die schöne Melusine
(Fair Melusine) Overture, op. 32
ISBN 3-7957-7110-2   ISMN M-2002-0526-8
ETP 606

Paulus / St. Paul
Overture to the Oratorio, op. 36
ISBN 3-7957-6352-5   ISMN M-2002-0591-6
ETP 684

Athalia
Overture, op. 74
ISMN M-2002-0590-9
ETP 683

Ruy Blas
Overture, op. 95
ISBN 3-7957-6985-X   ISMN M-2002-0531-2
ETP 611

Heimkehr aus der Fremde
(Son and Stranger), Overture, op. 89
ISMN M-2002-0589-3
ETP 682

Concertos

Piano Concerto No. 1 G minor
op. 25 (Alberti)
ISBN 3-7957-6869-1   ISMN M-2002-0696-8
ETP 795

Piano Concerto No. 2 D minor
op. 40 (Alberti)
ISBN 3-7957-6163-8   ISMN M-2002-1021-7
ETP 1267

Violin Concerto E minor
op. 64 (Alberti)
ISBN 3-7957-6630-3   ISMN M-2002-0604-3
ETP 702

Chamber Music

String Quartets
E♭ major, op. 12
ISBN 3-7957-6720-2   ISMN M-2002-0068-3
ETP 47

minor, op. 13
N 3-7957-6816-0   ISMN M-2002-0088-1
68

major, op. 44/1
N 3-7957-6614-1   ISMN M-2002-0069-0
48

minor, op. 44/2
N 3-7957-6799-7   ISMN M-2002-0030-0
7

minor, op. 80
N 3-7957-6271-5   ISMN M-2002-0121-5
101

major, op. 81
Four Pieces)
N 3-7957-6132-8   ISMN M-2002-0122-2
102

ring Quintet A major
2 violins, 2 violas and cello, op. 18
N M-2002-0143-7
134

ring Quintet B♭ major
2 violins, 2 violas and cello, op. 87
N 3-7957-6269-3   ISMN M-2002-0087-4
67

ctet E♭ major
4 violins, 2 violas and 2 cellos, op. 20
N 3-7957-7140-4   ISMN M-2002-0080-5
59

ano Trio D minor, op. 49
N 3-7957-6357-6   ISMN M-2002-0100-0
80

ano Trio C minor, op. 66/2
N 3-7957-6973-6   ISMN M-2002-0101-7
81

Monteverdi, Claudio
(1567-1643)

horal and Vocal Music

udate Dominum
ntata (Psalm 117) , M xv, 481
nold)
udy score (= vocal score)
MN M-2002-0912-9
P 1069

parate parts:
mbone I/II
MN M-2002-1695-0
97-11

mbone III/IV
MN M-2002-1696-7
97-12

lin I
MN M-2002-1697-4
97-13

---

violin II
ISMN M-2002-1698-1
PC 97-14

cello/double bass
ISMN M-2002-1699-8
PC 97-15

organ/harpsichord
ISMN M-2002-1700-1
PC 97-16

Magnificat
(Luk. 1, 46-55) , M xiv, 327 / SV 206, Anh.
(Arnold)
ISMN M-2002-0913-6
ETP 1071

Missa I
„In Illo Tempore" à 6 (1610) (Redlich)
study score (= vocal score)
ISMN M-2002-0837-5
ETP 991

Messa Nr. II in F
M xv, 59 (Arnold)
study score (= vocal score)
ISBN 3-7957-6627-3   ISMN M-2002-0836-8
ETP 990

Messa Nr. III in g
(1651), M xvi, 1 (Redlich)
study score (= vocal score)
ISMN M-2002-0829-0
ETP 982

Vespro della Beata Vergine
Marienvesper (1610), SV 206 (Roche)
study score
ISBN 3-7957-6962-0   ISMN M-2002-1187-0
ETP 8024

separate parts:
fifara I
ISMN M-2002-2283-8
EOS 8024-01

fifara II
ISMN M-2002-2284-5
EOS 8024-02

flauto I
ISMN M-2002-2285-2
EOS 8024-03

flauto II
ISMN M-2002-2286-9
EOS 8024-04

cornetto I
ISMN M-2002-2287-6
EOS 8024-05

cornetto II
ISMN M-2002-2288-3
EOS 8024-06

cornetto III
ISMN M-2002-2289-0
EOS 8024-07

trombone I
ISMN M-2002-2290-6
EOS 8024-08

trombone II
ISMN M-2002-2291-3
EOS 8024-09

---

trombone III
ISMN M-2002-2292-0
EOS 8024-10

violino da brazzo I
ISMN M-2002-2293-7
EOS 8024-11

violino da brazzo II
ISMN M-2002-2294-4
EOS 8024-12

viuola da brazzo I
ISMN M-2002-2295-1
EOS 8024-13

viuola da brazzo II
ISMN M-2002-2296-8
EOS 8024-14

viuola da brazzo III
ISMN M-2002-2297-5
EOS 8024-15

viuola da brazzo IV
ISMN M-2002-2298-2
EOS 8024-16

contrabasso da gamba
ISMN M-2002-2299-9
EOS 8024-17

instrumental cantus
ISMN M-2002-2300-2
EOS 8024-18

instrumental altus
ISMN M-2002-2301-9
EOS 8024-19

instrumental tenor
ISMN M-2002-2302-6
EOS 8024-20

instrumental bassus
ISMN M-2002-2303-3
EOS 8024-21

instrumental quintus
ISMN M-2002-2304-0
EOS 8024-22

instrumental sextus
ISMN M-2002-2305-7
EOS 8024-23

bassus generalis
ISMN M-2002-2306-4
EOS 8024-24

Opera

L'Orfeo
Favola in Musica, SV 318 (Gallico)
ISBN 3-7957-6986-8   ISMN M-2002-2061-2
ETP 8025

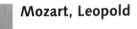

Mozart, Leopold

(1719-1787)

Sinfonia G major
(1753) (Landon)
study score
ISMN M-2002-0461-2
ETP 539

separate parts:

violin I/II
ISMN M-2002-1374-4
PC 42-11

viola
ISMN M-2002-1375-1
PC 42-12

cello/double bass
ISMN M-2002-1376-8
PC 42-13

harpsichord
ISMN M-2002-1377-5
PC 42-14

Sinfonia di caccia G major
"Jagdsinfonie" (Braun)
ISMN M-2002-0500-8
ETP 580

separate parts:

horn I/II in G
ISMN M-2002-1734-6
PC 106-11

horn III/IV in D
ISMN M-2002-1735-3
PC 106-12

shutgun / Kugelbüchse
ISMN M-2002-1736-0
PC 106-13

violin I
ISMN M-2002-1737-7
PC 106-14

violin II
ISMN M-2002-1738-4
PC 106-15

viola
ISMN M-2002-1739-1
PC 106-16

bassi
ISMN M-2002-1740-7
PC 106-17

Mozart, Wolfgang Amadeus
(1756-1791)
Choral and Vokal Works

Missa C major
"Piccolominimesse", K 258 (Schroeder)
ISMN M-2002-0795-8
ETP 944

Missa C major
"Krönungsmesse" / "Coronation Mass"
K 317 (Schroeder)
ISBN 3-7957-6128-X   ISMN M-2002-0818-4
ETP 971

Missa C minor
K 427/417a (Landon)
ISBN 3-7957-6277-4   ISMN M-2002-0830-6
ETP 983

Missa brevis D major
K 194 (Schroeder)
ISBN 3-7957-6165-4   ISMN M-2002-0832-0
ETP 986

Missa brevis C major
"Spatzen-Messe", K 220 (Schroeder)
ISBN 3-7957-6342-8   ISMN M-2002-0834-4
ETP 988

Regina coeli
K 276 (Schroeder)
ISMN M-2002-0925-9
ETP 1083

Requiem
D minor, K 626 (Blume)
ISBN 3-7957-6883-7   ISMN M-2002-0803-0
ETP 954

Exsultate, jubilate
Motet, K 165 (Einstein)
ISBN 3-7957-6184-0   ISMN M-2002-0865-8
ETP 1022

Litaniae Lauretanae
D major, K 195 (Schroeder)
ISMN M-2002-0794-1
ETP 943

Operas

Così fan tutte
(1789-90), K 588 (Redlich)
ISBN 3-7957-7122-6   ISMN M-2002-0786-6
ETP 920

Don Giovanni
(1787) K 527 (Einstein)
ISMN M-2002-0784-2
ETP 918

Die Entführung aus dem Serail
(The Abduction from the Seraglio)
(1781-82), K 384 (Redlich)
ISBN 3-7957-6997-3   ISMN M-2002-0785-9
ETP 919

Le Nozze di Figaro
(1785-86) (The Marriage of Figaro /
Die Hochzeit des Figaro), K 492
ISBN 3-7957-6308-8   ISMN M-2002-0782-8
ETP 916

Die Zauberflöte
(The Magic Flute) (1791), K 620 (Abert)
ISBN 3-7957-6954-X   ISMN M-2002-0778-1
ETP 912

Orchestral Works

Symphonies
No. 25, G minor, K 183
(1773-74) (Redlich)
ISBN 3-7957-6705-9   ISMN M-2002-0469-8
ETP 547

No. 28, C major, K 200
(1774) (Redlich)
ISMN M-2002-0470-4
ETP 548

No. 29 A major, K 201
(1774) (Cudworth)
ISBN 3-7957-6334-7   ISMN M-2002-0468-1
ETP 546

No. 30 D major, K 202
(1774) (Sadie)
ISMN M-2002-0498-8
ETP 578

No. 31 D major, K 297
"Paris" – with alternative 2nd movement
(1778) (Redlich)
ISBN 3-7957-6288-X   ISMN M-2002-0463-6
ETP 541

No. 33 B♭ major, K 319
(1779) (Redlich)
ISMN M-2002-0465-0
ETP 543

No. 34 C major, K 338
with Menuet K 409 (1780) (Redlich)
ISMN M-2002-0464-3
ETP 542

No. 35 D major, K 385
"Haffner" (1782) (Kroyer)
ISBN 3-7957-7150-1   ISMN M-2002-0374-5
ETP 437

No. 36 C major, K 425
"Linzer" (1783) (Kroyer)
ISMN M-2002-0429-2
ETP 502

No. 38 D major, K 504
"Prague" – without Menuet (1786) (Kroyer)
ISBN 3-7957-6868-3   ISMN M-2002-0383-7
ETP 446

No. 39 E♭ major, K 543
(1788) (Kroyer)
ISBN 3-7957-6700-8   ISMN M-2002-0352-3
ETP 415

No. 40 G Minor, K 550
(1788) (Woodham)
ISBN 3-7957-6697-4   ISMN M-2002-0341-7
ETP 404

No. 41 C major, K 551
„Jupiter" (1788) (Haan)
ISBN 3-7957-6696-6   ISMN M-2002-0338-7
ETP 401

La Clemenza di Tito
Overture, K 621 (Gerber)
ISBN 3-7957-6355-X   ISMN M-2002-0573-2
ETP 660

Così fan tutte
Overture, K 588 (Gerber)
ISMN M-2002-0575-6
ETP 662

Don Giovanni
Overture, K 527 (Einstein)
ISBN 3-7957-6994-9   ISMN M-2002-0528-2
ETP 608

e Entführung aus dem Serail
erture, K 384 (Gerber)
N 3-7957-6995-7   ISMN M-2002-0576-3
 663

omeneo Rè di Creta
erture, K 366 (Gerber)
N M-2002-0574-9
 661

 Nozze di Figaro
erture to the Opera, K 492 (Abert)
N 3-7957-6661-3   ISMN M-2002-0523-7
 603

er Schauspieldirektor
e Impressario)
fonia (Overture) to the Comedy with Music in
ct, K 486
N 3-7957-6982-5   ISMN M-2002-0952-5
 1119

ie Zauberflöte
erture, K 620
N 3-7957-6855-1   ISMN M-2002-0534-3
 614

aurerische Trauermusik
asonic Funeral Music), K 477
N M-2002-0725-5
 830

es petits riens
let Music, K 299b
N 3-7957-6290-1   ISMN M-2002-0736-1
 854

oncertos

iano Concertos
. 5 D major, K 175
h Rondo D major, K 382 (1773)
adura-Skoda)
N M-2002-1024-8
 1270

. 6 B♭ major, K 238
denzas by the composer (1776) (Badura-
oda)
N 3-7957-6246-4   ISMN M-2002-1020-0
 1266

. 8 C major, K 246
itzow" (1776) (Badura-Skoda)
N M-2002-1023-1
 1269

. 9 E♭ major, K 271
eunehomme" (1777) (Blume)
N 3-7957-6804-7   ISMN M-2002-0643-2
 742

. 11 F major, K 413
denzas by the composer (1782/83) (Redlich)
N 3-7957-6362-2   ISMN M-2002-0973-0
 1208

. 12 A major, K 414
82) (Badura-Skoda)
N 3-7957-6849-7   ISMN M-2002-0701-9
 800

No. 13 C major, K 415
(1782/83) (Redlich)
ISMN M-2002-0971-6
ETP 1206

No. 14 E♭ major, K 449
(1784) (Redlich)
ISMN M-2002-0969-3
ETP 1204

No. 15 B♭ major, K 450
(1784) (Köhler)
ISMN M-2002-0644-9
ETP 743

No. 16 D major, K 451
Cadenzas by the composer (1784) (Redlich)
ISMN M-2002-0972-3
ETP 1207

No. 17 G major, K 453
(1784) (Blume)
ISBN 3-7957-6923-X   ISMN M-2002-0661-6
ETP 760

No. 18 B♭ major, K 456
Cadenzas by the composer (1784) (Redlich)
ISMN M-2002-0697-5
ETP 796

No. 19 F major, K 459
Coronation I / Krönungs-Konzert I
Cadenzas by the composer (1784)
ISBN 3-7957-7143-9   ISMN M-2002-0662-3
ETP 761

No. 20 D minor, K 466
(1785) (Badura-Skoda)
ISBN 3-7957-6885-3   ISMN M-2002-0623-4
ETP 721

No. 21 C major, K 467
(1785) (Blume)
ISBN 3-7957-6666-4   ISMN M-2002-0640-1
ETP 739

No. 22 E♭ major, K 482
(1785) (Blume)
ISBN 3-7957-6864-0   ISMN M-2002-0638-8
ETP 737

No. 23 A major, K 488
(1786) (Blume)
ISBN 3-7957-6644-3   ISMN M-2002-0637-1
ETP 736

No. 24 C minor, K 491
Cadenzas by the composer (1786) (Blume)
ISMN M-2002-0641-8
ETP 740

No. 25 C major, K 503
(1786) (Blume/Matthews)
ISMN M-2002-0675-3
ETP 774

No. 26 D major, K 537
Coronation II / Krönungs-Konzert II
(1788) (Blume)
ISBN 3-7957-7136-6   ISMN M-2002-0621-0
ETP 719

No. 27 B♭ major, K 595
(1791) (Blume)
ISBN 3-7957-6847-0   ISMN M-2002-0676-0
ETP 775

Concert Rondo D major
for piano and orchestra, K 382 (1782) (Junk)
ISBN 3-7957-6871-3   ISMN M-2002-0684-5
ETP 783

Concerto E♭ major
for 2 pianos and orchestra, K 365
(1779) (Badura-Skoda)
ISBN 3-7957-6631-1   ISMN M-2002-0642-5
ETP 741

Violin Concertos
(1775) (Gerber)
B♭ major, K 207
ISMN M-2002-0664-7
ETP 763

D major, K 211
ISMN M-2002-0665-4
ETP 764

G major, K 216
ISBN 3-7957-6621-4   ISMN M-2002-0648-7
ETP 747

D major, K 218
ISBN 3-7957-6931-0   ISMN M-2002-0649-4
ETP 748

A major, K 219
ISBN 3-7957-6750-4   ISMN M-2002-0619-7
ETP 717

E♭ major, K 268
(1780)
ISMN M-2002-0620-3
ETP 718

Concertone C major
for 2 violins and orchestra, K 190
(1773) (Sadie)
ISMN M-2002-1004-0
ETP 1249

Flute Concerto G major
K 313 (1778) (Gerber)
ISBN 3-7957-6902-7   ISMN M-2002-0680-7
ETP 779   (L)

Flute Concerto D major
K 314 (1778) (Gerber)
ISBN 3-7957-6632-X   ISMN M-2002-0672-2
ETP 771

Clarinet Concerto A major
K 622 (1791) (Gerber)
ISBN 3-7957-6667-2   ISMN M-2002-0679-1
ETP 778

Basson Concerto B♭ major
K 191 (1774) (Junk)
ISBN 3-7957-6936-1   ISMN M-2002-0685-2
ETP 784

Horn Concertos

(Merian)

No. 1 D major, K 412
with Facsimile of Fragment (K 494a) (1774)
ISBN 3-7957-6937-X ISMN M-2002-0700-2
ETP 799

No. 2 E♭ major, K 417
(1783)
ISMN M-2002-0693-7
ETP 792

No. 3 E♭ major, K 447
(1783)
ISBN 3-7957-6150-6 ISMN M-2002-0690-6
ETP 789

No. 4 E♭ major, K 495
(1783)
ISBN 3-7957-6274-X ISMN M-2002-0698-2
ETP 797

Concerto C major

for flute, harp and orchestra, K 299
(1778) (Gerber)
ISBN 3-7957-6852-7 ISMN M-2002-0668-5
ETP 767

Sinfonia concertante E♭ major

for violin, viola and orchestra, K 364
(1779) (Gerber)
ISMN M-2002-0636-4
ETP 734

Sinfonia concertante E♭ major

for oboe, clarinet, horn, bassoon and strings, K
297b / K Anh. I Nr. 9 (1778) (Blume)
ISBN 3-7957-6841-1 ISMN M-2002-0656-2
ETP 755

Serenades and Divertimentos

Eine kleine Nachtmusik

Serenade G major, K 525 (1787) (Rexroth)
ISBN 3-7957-6111-5 ISMN M-2002-0212-0
ETP 218

set of parts soloistically
(1 violin I, 1 violin II, 1 viola, 2 cellos and bass)
ISMN M-2002-1808-4
EOS 218-10

set of parts in groups
(3 violins I, 3 violins II, 2 violas,
3 cellos/double basses)
ISMN M-2002-1807-7
EOS 218-70

separate parts:
violin I
ISMN M-2002-1824-4
EOS 218-11
violin II
ISMN M-2002-1825-1
EOS 218-12
viola
ISMN M-2002-1826-8
EOS 218-13
cello/double bass
ISMN M-2002-1827-5
EOS 218-14

Serenades

No. 3 D major, K 185 (Finalmusik)
and March, K 189
"Antretter-Serenade" (1773) (Sadie)
ISBN 3-7957-6323-1 ISMN M-2002-1062-0
ETP 1330

No. 4 D major , K 203
and March, K 237
(1774) (Sadie)
ISMN M-2002-1071-2
ETP 1341

No. 6 D major, K 239
"Serenade notturna"
for 2 small orchestras (1776) (Gerber)
ISBN 3-7957-6990-6 ISMN M-2002-0741-5
ETP 859

No. 7 D major, K 250
"Haffner Serenade"
for violin and orchestra (1776) (Gerber)
ISBN 3-7957-6321-5 ISMN M-2002-0239-7
ETP 262

No. 8 D major, K 286
"Notturno" (1776/77) (Gerber)
for 4 small orchestras
ISBN 3-7957-7144-7 ISMN M-2002-0740-8
ETP 858

No. 9 D major, K 320
und 2 Marches, K 335
"Posthorn-Serenade" (1779) (Landon)
ISBN 3-7957-6131-X ISMN M-2002-1053-8
ETP 1311

No. 10 B♭ major, K 361
"Gran Partita" for 12 wind instruments and
double bass (1781) (Newstone)

study score
ISBN 3-7957-6768-7 ISMN M-2002-1916-6
ETP 100

set of parts
ISMN M-2002-1915-9
ECS 100-60

No. 11 E♭ major, K 375
for 2 french horns, 2 oboes, 2 clarinets and 2
bassoons (1781) (Newstone)

study score
ISBN 3-7957-6636-2 ISMN M-2002-0276-2
ETP 308

set of parts
ISMN M-2002-1917-3
ECS 308-60   i.V. / in prep.

No. 12 C minor, K 388
"Nacht Musique" / "Night Music"
for 2 horns, 2 oboes, 2 clarinets in B♭ and
2 bassoons (1782) (Newstone)

study score
ISBN 3-7957-6919-1 ISMN M-2002-0277-9
ETP 309

set of parts
ISMN M-2002-1995-1
ECS 309-60

Divertimentos

No. 7 D major, K 205
for 2 french horns, violin, viola, bassoon and
bass (1773)
ISMN M-2002-0147-5
ETP 141

No. 8 F major, K 213
for 2 oboes, 2 horns and 2 bassoons
(1775) (Braun)
ISBN 3-7957-6316-9 ISMN M-2002-0332-5
ETP 394

No. 9 B♭ major, K 240
for 2 oboes, 2 horns and 2 bassoons
(1776) (Braun)
ISMN M-2002-0333-2
ETP 395

No. 10 F major, K 247
and March, K 248
1. Lodronische Nachtmusik
for 2 french horns, 2 violins, viola and bass
(1776) (Merian)
ISMN M-2002-0201-4
ETP 195

No. 11 D major, K 251
for oboe, 2 horns, 2 violins, viola and bass
(1776) (Landon)
ISMN M-2002-0294-6
ETP 349

No. 12 E♭ major, K 252
for 2 oboes, 2 french horns and 2 bassoons
(1776) (Braun)
ISMN M-2002-0334-9
ETP 396

No. 13 F major, K 253
for 2 oboes, 2 horns and 2 bassoons (1776)
ISMN M-2002-0295-3
ETP 351

No. 14 B♭ major, K 270
for 2 oboes, 2 horns and 2 bassoons (1777)
ISMN M-2002-0296-0
ETP 352

No. 15 B♭ major, K 287
for 2 violins, viola, double bass and 2 horns
(1777) (Gerber)
ISBN 3-7957-6800-4 ISMN M-2002-0093-5
ETP 73

No. 17 D major, K 334
for 2 violins, viola, double bass and 2 horns
(1779) (Gerber)
ISMN M-2002-0092-8
ETP 72

Ein musikalischer Spaß, K 522

(A Musical Joke) F major
"Dorfmusikanten-Sextett"
for 2 horns and string quartet (1787) (Redlich)
ISBN 3-7957-6694-X ISMN M-2002-0211-3
ETP 217

amber Music

agio and Fugue C minor
strings, K 546 (1788) (Redlich)

dy score
N M-2002-0311-0
369

of parts soloistically
N M-2002-1879-4
369-10

of parts in groups
olins I, 3 violins II, 2 violas,
llos/double basses)
N M-2002-1884-8
369-70

arate parts:

n I
N M-2002-1880-0
369-11

n II
N M-2002-1881-7
369-12

a
N M-2002-1882-4
369-13

/double bass
N M-2002-1883-1
369-14

agio and Rondo
glass harmonica, flute, oboe, viola and cello
1), K 617 (Salter)
N M-2002-1123-8
1402

vertimento E♭ major
for violin, viola and cello, K 563
88) (Gerber)
N 3-7957-6845-4   ISMN M-2002-0090-4
70

ring Quartets
die)

najor, K 387
32)
N 3-7957-6836-5   ISMN M-2002-0025-6
1

ninor, K 421
33)
N 3-7957-6831-4   ISMN M-2002-0054-6
32

najor, K 428
43)
N M-2002-0055-3
33

najor, K 458
gd-Quartett" / "Hunt" (1784)
N 3-7957-6872-1   ISMN M-2002-0056-0
34

najor, K 464
uken-Quartett" (1785)
N 3-7957-6972-8   ISMN M-2002-0057-7
35

C major, K 465
"Dissonanzen-Quartett" (1785)
ISMN M-2002-0031-7
ETP 8

D major, K 499
(1786)
ISMN M-2002-0046-1
ETP 24

"Preußische Quartette" / "Prussian Quartets"
D major, K 575
(1789)
ISBN 3-7957-6867-5   ISMN M-2002-0047-8
ETP 25

B♭ major, K 589
(1790)
ISMN M-2002-0048-5
ETP 26

F major, K 590
(1790)
ISBN 3-7957-6963-9   ISMN M-2002-0049-2
ETP 27

String Quintets
for 2 violins, 2 violas and cello
B♭ major, K 174
(1773) (Woodham)
ISMN M-2002-1122-1
ETP 1401

C minor, K 406
arranged from Serenade No. 12 (K 388)
(1787) (Gerber)
ISMN M-2002-0059-1
ETP 37

C major, K 515
(1787) (Gerber)
ISBN 3-7957-6360-6   ISMN M-2002-0060-7
ETP 38

G minor, K 516
(1787) (Gerber)
ISBN 3-7957-6649-4   ISMN M-2002-0036-2
ETP 13

D major, K 593
(1790) (Gerber)
ISMN M-2002-0071-3
ETP 50

E♭ major, K 614
(1791) (Gerber)
ISMN M-2002-0072-0
ETP 51

Piano Quartet G minor, K 478
for piano, violin, viola and cello
(1785) (Fiske)
ISBN 3-7957-7105-6   ISMN M-2002-0164-2
ETP 158

Piano Quartet E♭ major, K 493
for piano, violin, viola and cello
(1786) (Redlich)
ISMN M-2002-0165-9
ETP 159

Quintet E♭ major, K 452
for piano, oboe, clarinet, horn and bassoon
(1784) (Husmann)
ISBN 3-7957-6625-7   ISMN M-2002-0166-6
ETP 160

Quartet D major, K 285
for flute, violin, viola and cello (1777)
ISBN 3-7957-6905-1   ISMN M-2002-0198-7
ETP 192

Quartet A major, K 298
for flute, violin, viola and cello (1778)
ISBN 3-7957-6675-3   ISMN M-2002-0199-4
ETP 193

Quartet F major, K 370
for oboe, violin, viola and cello
(1781) (Husmann)
ISMN M-2002-0200-7
ETP 194

Quintet A major, K581
for clarinet, 2 violins, viola and cello
(1789) (Gerber)
ISBN 3-7957-6915-9   ISMN M-2002-0091-1
ETP 71

Quintet E♭ major, K 407
for horn, violin, 2 violas and cello
(1789) (Gerber)
ISBN 3-7957-6286-3   ISMN M-2002-0292-2
ETP 347

Trio E♭ major, K 498
"Kegelstatt-Trio"
for piano, clarinet and viola (Redlich)
ISBN 3-7957-6605-2   ISMN M-2002-0314-1
ETP 376

Mussorgsky, Modest Petrovich
(1839-1881)

Khovanshchina
Introduction to the Opera
ISMN M-2002-0599-2
ETP 695

Night on the Bare Mountain
(Eine Nacht auf dem kahlen Berge)
Orchestrated by Rimsky-Korsakoff
(Abraham)
ISMN M-2002-0732-3
ETP 841

Pictures at an Exhibition
(Bilder einer Ausstellung)
Instrumentation by Maurice Ravel
ISMN M-2002-2049-0
ETP 8022

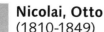

Nicolai, Otto
(1810-1849)

Die lustigen Weiber von Windsor
(The Merry Wives of Windsor)
Overture to the Opera
ISMN M-2002-0535-0
ETP 615

Nono, Luigi
(1924-1990)

Il canto sospeso
Cantate (Brieftexte europäischer Widerstandskämpfer)
ISMN M-2002-1812-1
ETP 8029   (L)

Nussio, Otmar
(1902-1990)

Escapades Musicales
for orchestra (1949)
ISMN M-2002-0767-5
ETP 900   (L)

Orff, Carl
(1895-1982)

Carmina Burana
Cantiones profanae (1936) (Thomas)
ISBN 3-7957-6237-5   ISMN M-2002-1167-2
ETP 8000   (L)

Catulli Carmina
Ludi scaenici – Szenische Spiele (1943)
ISBN 3-7957-6318-5   ISMN M-2002-1179-5
ETP 8015   (L)

Trionfo di Afrodite
Concerto scenico (1951)
ISMN M-2002-1180-1
ETP 8016   (L)

Tanzende Faune
An Orchestral Play, op. 21 (1914) (Hauschka)
ISBN 3-7957-6224-3   ISMN M-2002-2006-3
ETP 1459   (L)

Pachelbel, Johann
(1653-1706)

Canon e Gigue
(Beechey)
study score
ISBN 3-7957-6860-8   ISMN M-2002-2007-0
ETP 1411

---

set of string parts
(3 violin I, 3 violin II, 3 violin III, 3 cellos)
ISMN M-2002-2012-4
EOS 1411-70

separate parts:
violin I
ISMN M-2002-2018-6
EOS 1411-11
violin II
ISMN M-2002-2019-3
EOS 1411-12
violin III
ISMN M-2002-2021-6
EOS 1411-16
basso
ISMN M-2002-2020-9
EOS 1411-14
basso continuo
ISBN 3-7957-6912-4   ISMN M-2002-2011-7
EOS 1411-65

Palestrina, Giovanni Pierluigi da
(c. 1525-1594)

Missa Papae Marcelli
ISBN 3-7957-6281-2   ISMN M-2002-0811-5
ETP 963

Stabat mater
ISBN 3-7957-6361-4   ISMN M-2002-0814-6
ETP 966

Pergolesi, Giovanni Battista
(1710-1736)

Stabat mater
(Neubacher)
ISBN 3-7957-7109-9   ISMN M-2002-0820-7
ETP 973

Pfitzner, Hans
(1869-1949)

Von deutscher Seele, op. 28
(A German Soul) (Osthoff)
A Romantic cantata based on lines and poems by Josef von Eichendorff (1921)
ISBN 3-7957-6989-2   ISMN M-2002-2062-9
ETP 8065

Palestrina
Musical legend in 3 acts (1912-15)
ISMN M-2002-1189-4
ETP 8034   (L)

Symphony C minor
after the string quartet C♯ minor
for orchestra, op. 36a (1932)
ISMN M-2002-1137-5
ETP 1521

Piano Concerto E♭ major
op. 31 (1922)
ISMN M-2002-1162-7
ETP 1820   (L)

Violin Concerto B minor
in one movement, op. 34 (1923)
ISMN M-2002-1183-2
ETP 8019   (L)

Cello Concerto A minor
op. posth. (1888) (Osthoff)
ISMN M-2002-1163-4
ETP 1821   (L)

Praetorius, Michael
(1571-1621)

Wie schön leuchtet der Morgenstern
(How bright and fair the morning star)
Chorale Concert (1619) (Redlich)
ISMN M-2002-0888-7
ETP 1045

Prokofiev, Serge
(1891-1953)

Peter and the Wolf
A musical tale for children, op. 67
ISBN 3-7957-6258-8   ISMN M-2002-1114-6
ETP 1393   (L)

Purcell, Henry
(1659-1695)

Choral and Vocal Works

O Sing unto the Lord
Anthem, Z 44 (Arnold)
ISMN M-2002-0906-8
ETP 1063

Ode for St. Cecilia's Day 1683
"Welcome to all the pleasures"
(Selig, selig die Lust und Wonne) (Bergmann)
study score
ISBN 3-7957-6943-4   ISMN M-2002-0905-1
ETP 1062

separate parts:
violin I
EOS 1062-11
violin II
EOS 1062-12

a
S 1062-13

o/double bass
S 1062-14

sso continuo
MN M-2002-2313-2
S 1062-65

Deum and Jubilate
St. Cecilia's Day 1694, Z 232 (Arnold)

dy score
N 3-7957-6891-8   ISMN M-2002-0907-5
ᵖ 1064

parate parts:

mpet I
MN M-2002-2281-4
S 1064-44

mpet II
MN M-2002-2282-1
S 1064-45

in I
MN M-2002-2277-7
S 1064-11

in II
MN M-2002-2278-4
S 1064-12

la
MN M-2002-2279-1
S 1064-13

lo/double bass
MN M-2002-2280-7
S 1064-14

sso continuo
MN M-2002-2312-5
S 1064-06

peras

ido and Aeneas
arris)
N 3-7957-6837-3   ISMN M-2002-0791-0
ᵖ 929

e Fairy Queen
Feenkönigin (Burden)
N 3-7957-6341-X   ISMN M-2002-2310-1
ᵖ 8027   i.V. / in prep.

rchestral Works

e Fairy Queen
uites from the Opera (Reed)
MN M-2002-0761-3
ᵖ 891

hamber Music

acony
2 violins, viola and bass (Bergmann)
N 3-7957-6746-6   ISMN M-2002-1102-3
ᵖ 1381

ntazias and In Nomines
3-7 instruments (Ford)
N 3-7957-6737-7   ISMN M-2002-1066-8
ᵖ 1334

10 Sonatas in Four Parts
for 2 violins, basso and basso continuo
(Hogwood)
Nos. 1-6
ISBN 3-7957-6939-6   ISMN M-2002-1087-3
ETP 1362

Nos. 7-10
ISMN M-2002-1088-0
ETP 1363

12 Sonatas of Three Parts
for 2 violins, basso and basso continuo (Fiske)
Nos. 1-6
ISBN 3-7957-6938-8   ISMN M-2002-1079-8
ETP 1353

Nos. 7-12
ISMN M-2002-1080-4
ETP 1354

Quantz,
Johann Joachim
(1697-1773)

Concerto G major
for flute, strings and b.c. (Schroeder)
study score
ISMN M-2002-0975-4
ETP 1212
solo flute
ISMN M-2002-1399-7
PC 48-01
separate parts:
violin I
ISMN M-2002-1401-7
PC 48-12
violin II
ISMN M-2002-1402-4
PC 48-13
viola
ISMN M-2002-1403-1
PC 48-14
cello/double bass
ISMN M-2002-1404-8
PC 48-15
harpsichord
ISMN M-2002-1400-0
PC 48-11

Ravel, Maurice
(1875-1937)

Alborada del gracioso
for orchestra (Nichols)
ISMN M-2002-2048-3
ETP 8001   (L)

Une barque sur l'océan
for orchestra (Nichols)
ISBN 3-7957-6878-0   ISMN M-2002-2013-1
ETP 8002

Bolero
for orchestra (1928) (Orenstein)
ISMN M-2002-1186-3
ETP 8023   (L)

Pavane pour une infante
défunte
for small orchestra (1899)
ISBN 3-7957-6607-9   ISMN M-2002-1850-3
ETP 1335   (L)

Reger, Max
(1873-1916)

Orchestral Works

Variations and Fugue
on a Theme of Beethoven, op. 86 (Popp)
ISMN M-2002-1121-4
ETP 1400

Variations and Fugue
on a Theme of Johann Adam Hiller (Popp)
ISMN M-2002-0730-9
ETP 835

Variations and Fugue
on a Theme of Mozart
ISMN M-2002-0722-4
ETP 827

4 Tondichtungen, op. 128
(Four Tone Poems)
after Arnold Böcklin (Popp)
ISMN M-2002-1184-9
ETP 8020

Concertos

Concerto F minor
for piano and orchestra, op. 114 (Popp)
ISMN M-2002-1185-6
ETP 8021

Chamber Music

String Trio A minor, op. 77b
ISBN 3-7957-6348-7   ISMN M-2002-0263-2
ETP 288

String Trio D minor, op. 141b
ISMN M-2002-0280-9
ETP 313

String Quartet E♭ major
op. 109
ISBN 3-7957-6266-9   ISMN M-2002-0264-9
ETP 293

String Quartet F minor
op. 121
ISBN 3-7957-6235-9   ISMN M-2002-0281-6
ETP 314

Trios ("Serenades")
for flute, violin and viola
D major, op. 77a
ISBN 3-7957-6987-6   ISMN M-2002-0262-5
ETP 287

G major, op. 141a
ISBN 3-7957-6245-6 ISMN M-2002-0279-3
ETP 312

Quintet A major, op. 146
for clarinet and string quartet
ISBN 3-7957-6992-2 ISMN M-2002-0283-0
ETP 322

Rimsky-Korsakoff, Nicolai
(1844-1908)

Capriccio espagnol, op. 34
ISBN 3-7957-6888-8 ISMN M-2002-0733-0
ETP 842

Le Coq d'or
(The Golden Cockerel / Der goldene Hahn)
Suite from the Opera
ISMN M-2002-1100-9
ETP 1377

Voskresnaja uvestjura
(Russian Easter festival / Russische Ostern)
Overture, op. 36 (1888)
ISBN 3-7957-6960-4 ISMN M-2002-0597-8
ETP 692

Scheherazade
Symphonic Suite, op. 35
ISMN M-2002-0424-7
ETP 493

Rodrigo, Joaquín
(1901-1999)

A la busca del más allá
for orchestra (1977) (Calcraft)
ISMN M-2002-1130-6
ETP 1455

Concierto pastoral
for flute and orchestra (1977) (Calcraft)
ISBN 3-7957-6106-9 ISMN M-2002-1823-7
ETP 1825   (L)

Concierto de Aranjuez
for guitar and orchestra (1939)
ISBN 3-7957-6242-1 ISMN M-2002-1154-2
ETP 1809   (L)

Fantasía para un gentilhombre
for guitar and orchestra (1954) (Calcraft)
ISMN M-2002-1165-8
ETP 1823   (L)

Concierto Madrigal
for 2 guitars and orchestra (1966) (Calcraft)
ISMN M-2002-1166-5
ETP 1824   (L)

Concierto Andaluz
for 4 guitars and orchestra (1967) (Calcraft)
ISMN M-2002-1188-7
ETP 8026   (L)

Rossini, Gioacchino
(1792-1868)

Choral and Vocal Works

Stabat Mater
(Tomelleri)
ISBN 3-7957-6261-8 ISMN M-2002-0831-3
ETP 984

Overtures

La Cenerentola
(Cinderella / Aschenbrödel)
ISBN 3-7957-6307-X ISMN M-2002-0953-2
ETP 1120

Il Barbiere di Siviglia
(The Barber of Seville / Der Barbier von Sevilla)
ISBN 3-7957-6709-1 ISMN M-2002-0592-3
ETP 685

The Siege of Corinth
(Die Belagerung von Korinth) (Kirby)
ISMN M-2002-0957-0
ETP 1126

La Gazza Ladra
(The Thieving Magpie / Die diebische Elster)
ISMN M-2002-0593-0
ETP 686

L'Italiana in Algeri
(The Italian Girl in Algiers /
Die Italienerin in Algier)
ISBN 3-7957-6821-7 ISMN M-2002-0945-7
ETP 1110

La Scala di Seta
(The silken ladder / Die seidene Leiter)
ISBN 3-7957-6312-6 ISMN M-2002-0948-8
ETP 1113

Semiramide
ISBN 3-7957-6601-X ISMN M-2002-0568-8
ETP 654

Tancredi
ISMN M-2002-0569-5
ETP 655

Il Turco in Italia
(The Turc in Italy / Der Türke in Italien)
ISMN M-2002-0954-9
ETP 1121

Wilhelm Tell
(Salter)
ISBN 3-7957-7120-X ISMN M-2002-0536-7
ETP 616

Rózsa, Míklos
(1907-1995)

3 Hungarian Sketches
Capriccio, Pastorale e Danza, op. 14 (1958)
ISBN 3-7957-7147-1 ISMN M-2002-1052-1
ETP 1309

Saint-Saëns, Camille
(1835-1921)

Le Carnaval des animaux
(The Carnival of Animals /
Der Karneval der Tiere)
Zoologic fantasy (Aprahamian)
ISBN 3-7957-6673-7 ISMN M-2002-1095-8
ETP 1370

Concerto No. 1 A minor
for cello and orchestra, op. 33
ISBN 3-7957-6176-X ISMN M-2002-1036-1
ETP 1285

Satie, Erik
(1866-1925)

Gymnopédies
(No. 1 and 2 orchestrated by C. Debussy)
(Dickinson)
ISMN M-2002-1099-6
ETP 1376

Schönberg, Arnold
(1874-1951)

Moses und Aron
Opera (Schmidt)
ISBN 3-7957-6138-7 ISMN M-2002-1169-6
ETP 8004   (L)

Fünf Orchesterstücke
(Five Orchestral Pieces)
Original Version, op. 16
ISBN 3-7957-6130-1 ISMN M-2002-1060-6
ETP 1328

Schubert, Franz
(1797-1828)

Choral and Vokal Works

Mass No. 5 A♭ major, D 678
ISBN 3-7957-6233-2 ISMN M-2002-0821-4
ETP 974

Mass No. 6 E♭ major, D 950
ISBN 3-7957-6146-8 ISMN M-2002-0817-7
ETP 970

Orchestral Works

Symphonies
No. 1 D major, D 82
ISMN M-2002-0431-5
ETP 504

2 B♭ major, D 125
N 3-7957-6685-0 ISMN M-2002-0432-2
505

3 D major, D 200
N 3-7957-7149-8 ISMN M-2002-0433-9
506

4 C minor, D 417
agic" / "Tragische"
N M-2002-0434-6
507

5 B♭ major, D 485
N 3-7957-6287-1 ISMN M-2002-0435-3
508

6 C Major, D 589
e Kleine"
N 3-7957-6141-7 ISMN M-2002-0436-0
509

8 B minor, D 759
finished" / "Unvollendete" (Reichenberger)
N 3-7957-6278-2 ISMN M-2002-0340-0
403

9 C major, D 944
e Great" / "Die Große" (Fiske)
N 3-7957-6699-0 ISMN M-2002-0347-9
410

fonso and Estrella, D 759 A
rture, op. 69
N M-2002-0602-9
698

erabras, D 796
rture, op. 76 (1823)
N M-2002-0959-4
1129

verture in the Italian Style D
ajor, D 590
N M-2002-0960-0
1130

verture in the Italian Style C
ajor, D 591
N 3-7957-6762-8 ISMN M-2002-0961-7
1131

samunde, D 644
rture to the Melodrama "The Magic Harp"
26
N 3-7957-6365-7 ISMN M-2002-0555-8
636

samunde
r'acte and Ballet Music
N 3-7957-6977-9 ISMN M-2002-0715-6
817

oncertos

anderer-Fantasie, D 760
nscribed by Franz Liszt
piano and orchestra, op. 15
N M-2002-1047-7
1300   (L)

Chamber Music

String Quartets

E♭ major, op. 125/1, D 87
ISBN 3-7957-6738-5 ISMN M-2002-0138-3
ETP 120

D major, op. posth., D 94
ISMN M-2002-0297-7
ETP 353

B♭ major, op. 168, D 112
ISMN M-2002-0134-5
ETP 116

G minor, op. posth., D 173
ISBN 3-7957-6898-5 ISMN M-2002-0135-2
ETP 117

E major, op. 125/2, D 353
ISMN M-2002-0137-6
ETP 119

A minor, op. 29, D 804
"Rosamunde"
ISBN 3-7957-6679-6 ISMN M-2002-0062-1
ETP 40

D minor, op. posth., D 810
"Der Tod und das Mädchen" /
"Death and the Maiden"
ISBN 3-7957-6345-2 ISMN M-2002-0034-8
ETP 11

G major, op. 161, D 887
ISMN M-2002-0061-4
ETP 39

Quartettsatz C minor, D 705
(Quartet Movement) op. posth.
ISBN 3-7957-6327-4 ISMN M-2002-0298-4
ETP 354

String Quintet C major, D 956
for 2 violins, viola and 2 cellos, op. 163
ISBN 3-7957-6970-1 ISMN M-2002-0038-6
ETP 15

Piano Trio E♭ major, D 897
"Notturno", op. 148
ISBN 3-7957-6735-0 ISMN M-2002-0216-8
ETP 233

Piano Trio B♭ major, D 898
op. 99
ISMN M-2002-0104-8
ETP 84

Piano Trio E♭ major, D 929
op. 100
ISBN 3-7957-6778-4 ISMN M-2002-0105-5
ETP 85

Quintet A major, D 667
"Forellen-Quintett" / "The Trout", op. 114
ISBN 3-7957-6125-5 ISMN M-2002-0136-9
ETP 118

Octet F major, D 803
for 2 violins, viola, cello, double bass, clarinet,
horn and bassoon, op. 166
ISBN 3-7957-6957-4 ISMN M-2002-0081-2
ETP 60

Schütz, Heinrich
(1585-1672)

Historia der Auferstehung
Jesu Christi, SWV 50
(The Ressurection of Jesus Christ) (Stein)
ISMN M-2002-0827-6
ETP 980

Weihnachts-Historie, SWV 435
(Christmas Story) (Stein)
ISBN 3-7957-7127-7 ISMN M-2002-0828-3
ETP 981

Die sieben Worte Jesu Christi
(The Seven Words of Jesus Christi) (Stein)
ISBN 3-7957-6232-4 ISMN M-2002-0824-5
ETP 977

Matthäus-Passion, SWV 479
ISMN M-2002-0823-8
ETP 976

Lukas-Passion, SWV 480
(Stein)
ISBN 3-7957-6298-7 ISMN M-2002-0825-2
ETP 978

Johannes-Passion, SWV 481
(1550) (Stein)
ISBN 3-7957-6208-1 ISMN M-2002-0826-9
ETP 979

Schumann, Robert
(1810-1856)

Choral and Vocal Works

Tragödie
for soprano, tenor and orchestra (Appel)
ISMN M-2002-1147-4
ETP 1709   (L)

Orchestral Works

Symphonies
(Correll Roesner)

No. 1 B♭ major, op. 38
"Frühlingssinfonie" / "Spring Symphony"
ISBN 3-7957-6921-3 ISMN M-2002-0354-7
ETP 417

No. 2 C Major, op. 61
ISMN M-2002-0358-5
ETP 421

No. 3 E♭ major, op. 97
"Rheinische"
ISBN 3-7957-6653-2 ISMN M-2002-0345-5
ETP 408   (L)

No. 4 D minor, op. 120
ISBN 3-7957-6617-6 ISMN M-2002-0350-9
ETP 413

Overture, Scherzo and Finale
op. 52
ISBN 3-7957-6881-0 ISMN M-2002-0487-2
ETP 567   (L)

Genoveva
Overture, op. 81
ISMN M-2002-0562-6
ETP 647

Manfred
Overture, op. 115
ISBN 3-7957-6613-3   ISMN M-2002-0561-9
ETP 646

Concertos

Violin Concerto D minor
(1853) (Schünemann)
ISBN 3-7957-6984-1   ISMN M-2002-1164-1
ETP 1822   (L)

Cello Concerto A minor, op. 129
(1850)
ISBN 3-7957-6668-0   ISMN M-2002-0687-6
ETP 786

Piano Concerto A minor, op. 54
(1845) (Boetticher)
ISBN 3-7957-6189-1   ISMN M-2002-0609-8
ETP 707

Phantasie A minor
for piano and orchestra (Boetticher)
ISMN M-2002-1129-0
ETP 1454

Chamber Music

String Quartets, op. 41
No. 1 A minor
ISBN 3-7957-6650-8   ISMN M-2002-0094-2
ETP 74

No. 2 F major
ISBN 3-7957-7107-2   ISMN M-2002-0095-9
ETP 75

No. 3 A major
ISBN 3-7957-6748-2   ISMN M-2002-0096-6
ETP 76

Piano Trio D minor, op. 63
ISBN 3-7957-6886-1   ISMN M-2002-0106-2
ETP 86

Piano Trio F major, op. 80
ISMN M-2002-0107-9
ETP 87

Piano Trio A minor, op. 88
Fantasiestücke
ISBN 3-7957-6170-0   ISMN M-2002-0119-2
ETP 99

Piano Trio G minor, op. 110
ISMN M-2002-0108-6
ETP 88

Piano Quartet E♭ major, op. 47
ISBN 3-7957-6133-6   ISMN M-2002-0097-3
ETP 77

Piano Quintet E♭ major, op. 44
for piano, 2 violins, viola and cello (1842)
ISBN 3-7957-6356-8   ISMN M-2002-0098-0
ETP 78

Märchenerzählungen
(Fairy Tales), op. 132
for clarinet (violin), viola and piano (1953)
ISMN M-2002-0215-1
ETP 228

Scriabin, Alexander
(1872-1915)

Symphony No. 2 C minor, op. 29
ISMN M-2002-0430-8
ETP 503

Le Poème de l'extase, op. 54
ISBN 3-7957-6209-X   ISMN M-2002-0425-4
ETP 497

Prometheus, op. 60
The Poem of Fire (Bowers)
ISBN 3-7957-6925-6   ISMN M-2002-1173-3
ETP 8008

Concerto F minor, op. 20
for piano and orchestra
ISBN 3-7957-6811-X   ISMN M-2002-1037-8
ETP 1287

Shostakovich, Dimitry
(1906-1975)

Symphony No. 5 D minor
op. 47 (1937) (Schneider)
ISBN 3-7957-6234-0   ISMN M-2002-0499-5
ETP 579

String Quartets
No. 1 C major, op. 49 (1938)
ISBN 3-7957-6294-4   ISMN M-2002-0323-3
ETP 385

No. 2 A major, op. 68 (1944)
ISMN M-2002-0324-0
ETP 386

No. 5 B♭ major, op. 92 (1952)
ISBN 3-7957-6103-4   ISMN M-2002-0327-1
ETP 389

No. 7 F minor, op. 108 (1960)
ISBN 3-7957-6304-5   ISMN M-2002-0329-5
ETP 391

No. 8 C major, op. 110 (1960)
"Dresden"
ISBN 3-7957-6257-X   ISMN M-2002-0330-1
ETP 392

Sibelius, Jean
(1865-1957)

Violin Concerto D minor, op. 47
ISBN 3-7957-6251-0   ISMN M-2002-0671-5
ETP 770

String Quartet D minor
Voces intimae, op. 56
ISBN 3-7957-6203-0   ISMN M-2002-0265-6
ETP 294

Smetana, Bedřich
(1824-1884)

Orchestral Works

Má Vlast
(My Fatherland / Mein Vaterland)
Symphonic Poems
No. 1 Vyšehrad
ISBN 3-7957-6965-5   ISMN M-2002-0404-9
ETP 471

No. 2 Vltava (Moldau)
(Pospíšil)
ISBN 3-7957-6752-0   ISMN M-2002-0405-6
ETP 472

No. 3 Šárka
ISBN 3-7957-7132-3   ISMN M-2002-0406-3
ETP 473

No. 4
From Bohemia's Fields and Groves
(Aus Böhmens Hain und Flur)
ISBN 3-7957-6805-5   ISMN M-2002-0407-0
ETP 474

No. 5 Tábor
ISMN M-2002-0408-7
ETP 475

No. 6 Blaník
ISBN 3-7957-6641-9   ISMN M-2002-0409-4
ETP 476

Libussa
Overture
ISMN M-2002-0586-2
ETP 677

The Bartered Bride
(Die verkaufte Braut)
Overture to the Opera
ISMN M-2002-0577-0
ETP 664

Chamber Music

String Quartet E minor
From my life (Aus meinem Leben)
ISBN 3-7957-6239-1   ISMN M-2002-0252-6
ETP 275

String Quartet D minor
ISBN 3-7957-6320-7   ISMN M-2002-0259-5
ETP 284

ano Trio G minor, op. 15
N 3-7957-6353-3   ISMN M-2002-0289-2
● 335

Spohr, Louis
(1784-1859)

●ncerto No. 8 A minor, op. 47
modo di scena cantante"
violin and orchestra
vIN M-2002-0605-0
● 703

●ctet E major, op. 32
clarinet in A, 2 french horns (E), violin,
●olas, cello and double bass
●N 3-7957-6798-9   ISMN M-2002-0142-0
● 126

●net F major, op. 31
violin, viola, cello, double bass, flute, oboe,
●rinet and bassoon
●N 3-7957-6741-5   ISMN M-2002-0117-8
● 97

Stamitz, Carl
(1745-1801)

●olin Concerto G major
●dy score
vIN M-2002-0974-7
●P 1210
●lo violin
vIN M-2002-1405-5
49-01
●nd band parts (2 flutes, 2 horns)
vIN M-2002-1406-2
49-10
●parate parts:
●lin I
vIN M-2002-1407-9
49-11
●lin II
vIN M-2002-1408-6
49-12
●la I/II
vIN M-2002-1409-3
49-13
●lo/double bass
vIN M-2002-1410-9
49-14

Stamitz, Johann
(1717-1801)

●arinet Concerto B♭ major
vIN M-2002-1044-6
● 1297

Flute Concerto D major
study score
ISMN M-2002-0995-2
ETP 1240
solo flute
ISMN M-2002-1559-5
PC 73-01
separate parts:
violin I
ISMN M-2002-1560-1
PC 73-11
violin II
ISMN M-2002-1561-8
PC 73-12
cello/double bass
ISMN M-2002-1562-5
PC 73-13

Strauß, Johann
(1825-1899)

Opera
Die Fledermaus / The Bat
Operetta in 3 Acts, op. 362 (Swarowsky)
ISBN 3-7957-6268-5   ISMN M-2002-0787-3
ETP 922   (L)

Orchestral Works
Die Fledermaus
Overture to the Operetta (Swarowsky)
ISBN 3-7957-6112-3   ISMN M-2002-0938-9
ETP 1103

Der Zigeunerbaron
Overture (Keldorfer)
ISBN 3-7957-6166-2   ISMN M-2002-0941-9
ETP 1106

Waltzes
(Keldorfer)
An der schönen blauen Donau
(The blue Danube), op. 314 (1867)
ISBN 3-7957-6211-1   ISMN M-2002-0718-7
ETP 822

Künstlerleben
(Artist's Life), op. 316 (1867)
ISMN M-2002-0749-1
ETP 870

Geschichten aus dem Wienerwald
(Tales from the Vienna Woods) op. 325 (1868)
ISBN 3-7957-6240-5   ISMN M-2002-0747-7
ETP 868

Wein, Weib und Gesang
(Wine, Women and Song), op. 333 (1869)
ISMN M-2002-0745-3
ETP 866

Wiener Blut
(Vienna Blood), op. 354 (1873)
ISBN 3-7957-6167-0   ISMN M-2002-0753-8
ETP 875

Rosen aus dem Süden
(Roses from the South) (1880)
Waltzes after "Das Spitzentuch der Königin",
op. 388
ISBN 3-7957-6310-X   ISMN M-2002-0746-0
ETP 867

Frühlingsstimmen
(Voices of Spring), op. 410 (1885)
ISMN M-2002-0748-4
ETP 869

Kaiserwalzer
op. 437 (1889)
ISBN 3-7957-6306-1   ISMN M-2002-0750-7
ETP 871

Strauss, Richard
(1864-1949)

Orchestral Works
Eine Alpensinfonie
op. 64, TrV 233 (Kohler)
ISBN 3-7957-6101-8   ISMN M-2002-1819-0
ETP 8046

Concert Overture C minor
o. op., AV 80 (1883) (Kohler)
ISMN M-2002-0965-5
ETP 1135   (L)

**Tanzsuite nach
François Couperin**
o. op., AV 107
ISMN M-2002-1128-3
ETP 1453

Symphonic Poems
Also sprach Zarathustra, op. 30
ISBN 3-7957-6656-7   ISMN M-2002-0381-3
ETP 444

Don Juan, op. 20
ISBN 3-7957-6703-2   ISMN M-2002-0377-6
ETP 440

Don Quixote, op. 35
ISBN 3-7957-6657-5   ISMN M-2002-0382-0
ETP 445

Ein Heldenleben, op. 40
(A Hero's Life) (Seifert)
ISBN 3-7957-6684-2   ISMN M-2002-0426-1
ETP 498

Macbeth, op. 23
ISMN M-2002-0378-3
ETP 441

Symphonia domestica, op. 53
ISMN M-2002-0437-7
ETP 510

Till Eulenspiegels lustige Streiche
op. 28
ISBN 3-7957-6619-2   ISMN M-2002-0380-6
ETP 443

Tod und Verklärung, op. 24
(Death and Transfiguration)
ISBN 3-7957-6814-4 ISMN M-2002-0379-0
ETP 442

Concertos

Burleske D minor
for piano and orchestra, o. op., AV 85,
TrV 145 (Kennedy)
ISBN 3-7957-6322-3 ISMN M-2002-1816-9
ETP 8045

Romanze E♭ major
for clarinet and orchestra, o. op. (1879),
AV 61 (Kohler)
ISBN 3-7957-6148-4 ISMN M-2002-1893-0
ETP 1458   (L)

Romanze F major
for cello and orchestra, o. op. (1883)
AV 75 (Kohler)
ISMN M-2002-1120-7
ETP 1399   (L)

Chamber Music

Suite B♭ major
for 13 wind instruments, op. 4
ISMN M-2002-1127-6
ETP 1410

Stravinsky, Igor
(1882-1971)

Orchestral Works

Symphony in C
(1940) (Karallus)
ISBN 3-7957-6229-4 ISMN M-2002-1134-4
ETP 1511   (L)

Symphony in 3 Movements
(1945) (Karallus)
ISBN 3-7957-6255-3 ISMN M-2002-0494-0
ETP 574   (L)

Concerto in E♭
"Dumbarton Oaks"
for chamber orchestra (1937-38)
ISBN 3-7957-6157-3 ISMN M-2002-1156-6
ETP 1813   (L)

Fireworks
Fantasy for orchestra, op. 4 (1908) (Schneider)
ISBN 3-7957-6158-1 ISMN M-2002-1117-7
ETP 1396   (L)

Jeu De Cartes
Ballet in three "deals" /
Ballett in drei "Runden" (1936) (Schneider)
ISBN 3-7957-6147-6 ISMN M-2002-1113-9
ETP 1392   (L)

L'oiseau de feu
(The Firebird / Der Feuervogel)
Ballet (1909-10) (Schneider)
ISBN 3-7957-6100-X ISMN M-2002-1818-3
ETP 8043   (L)

L'oiseau de feu
Ballet Suite 1945 (Schneider)
ISBN 3-7957-6238-3 ISMN M-2002-1110-8
ETP 1389   (L)

Scherzo à la Russe
Symphonic Version (1945) (Flamm)
ISBN 3-7957-6105-0 ISMN M-2002-1814-5
ETP 8035   (L)

Version for Jazz ensemble (1944) (Flamm)
ISBN 3-7957-6102-6 ISMN M-2002-1822-0
ETP 8049   (L)

Scherzo fantastique
"Der Bienenflug", op. 3 (1907-08) (Schneider)
ISMN M-2002-1181-8
ETP 8017

Concertos

Concerto en Ré
for violin and orchestra (1931) (Karallus)
ISBN 3-7957-6228-6 ISMN M-2002-1158-0
ETP 1815   (L)

Sullivan, Arthur
(1842-1900)

The Gondoliers
Comic Opera (Lloyd-Jones)
ISMN M-2002-0790-3
ETP 927

The Yeomen of the Guard
Overture
ISMN M-2002-0964-8
ETP 1134

Suppé,
Franz von
(1819-1895)

Dichter und Bauer
(Poet and Peasant)
Overture to the Vaudeville-Operetta
ISMN M-2002-0587-9
ETP 678

Tchaikovsky,
Peter Ilyich
(1840-1893)

Orchestral works

Symphonies
No. 1 G minor, op. 13
"Winter Reveries" / "Winterträume" (1874),
CW 21
ISBN 3-7957-6707-5 ISMN M-2002-0480-3
ETP 560

No. 2 C minor, op. 17
"Little Russian" / "Kleinrussische"
CW 22 (Abraham)
ISBN 3-7957-6706-7 ISMN M-2002-0475-9
ETP 555

No. 3 D major, op. 29
"Polish" / "Polnische"
(1875), CW 23 (Abraham)
ISBN 3-7957-6660-5 ISMN M-2002-0473-5
ETP 552

No. 4 F minor, op. 36
(1876-77), CW 24, based on the Soviet
Complete Collected Edition (Lloyd-Jones)
ISBN 3-7957-6655-9 ISMN M-2002-0367-7
ETP 430

No. 5 E minor, op. 64
(1888), CW 26 (Lloyd-Jones)
ISBN 3-7957-6832-2 ISMN M-2002-0366-0
ETP 429

No. 6 B minor, op. 74
"Pathétique" (1893), CW 27 (Lloyd-Jones)
ISBN 3-7957-6683-4 ISMN M-2002-0411-7
ETP 479

Manfred Symphony
op. 58 (1885), CW 25 (Abraham)
ISBN 3-7957-6757-1 ISMN M-2002-0427-8
ETP 500

La Belle au Bois Dormant
(The Sleeping Beauty / Dornröschen)
Suite from the Ballet, op. 66a (Lloyd-Jones)
ISBN 3-7957-6692-3 ISMN M-2002-1061-3
ETP 1329

Casse-Noisette
(The Nutcracker / Der Nussknacker)
Suite from the Ballet, op. 71a (Unger)
ISBN 3-7957-6729-6 ISMN M-2002-0720-0
ETP 824

Le Lac des Cygnes
(Swan Lake / Schwanensee), op. 20
Ballet Suite (1875-76), CW 13 (Priory)
ISBN 3-7957-6213-8 ISMN M-2002-1067-5
ETP 1336

Capriccio Italien
(1880), op. 45, CW 44
ISBN 3-7957-6624-9 ISMN M-2002-0703-2
ETP 802

Francesca da Rimini
Symphonic fantasia after Dante, op. 32 (1876
CW 43 (Lloyd-Jones)
ISMN M-2002-0731-6
ETP 840

1812
Overture solenelle (1880), op. 49
ISBN 3-7957-6775-X ISMN M-2002-0544-2
ETP 624

Hamlet, op. 67a
Fantasy Overture (1888), CW 50 (Abraham)
ISMN M-2002-0949-5
ETP 1115

...meo and Juliet
...tasy Overture, CW 39
...N 3-7957-6664-8   ISMN M-2002-0584-8
● 675

...renade C major
...strings, op. 48
...N 3-7957-6787-3   ISMN M-2002-0739-2
● 857

...avonic March, op. 31
...76), CW 42
...N 3-7957-6952-3   ISMN M-2002-0734-7
● 851

...ite No. 3 G major, op. 55
...N M-2002-1093-4
● 1368

...ite No. 4 G major, op. 61
...zartiana (1887), CW 31   (Unger)
...N 3-7957-6835-7   ISMN M-2002-0744-6
● 863

oncertos

...ano Concerto No. 1 B♭ minor
...23 (1874-75), CW 53   (Abraham)
...N 3-7957-6896-9   ISMN M-2002-0611-1
● 709

...ano Concerto No. 2 G major
...44 (1879-80), CW 55   (Lloyd-Jones)
...N 3-7957-6358-4   ISMN M-2002-0998-3
● 1243

...olin Concerto D major
...35 (1878), CW 54 (Abraham)
...N 3-7957-7119-6   ISMN M-2002-0610-4
● 708

...ariations on a Rococo Theme
...cello and orchestra, op. 33 (1876)
...N 3-7957-6156-5   ISMN M-2002-0689-0
● 788

...hamber Music

...tring Quartet No. 1 D major
...871), op. 11, CW 90
...N 3-7957-6600-1   ISMN M-2002-0167-3
● 161

...tring Quartet No. 2 F major
...874), op. 22, CW 91
...N 3-7957-6806-3   ISMN M-2002-0202-1
● 196

...tring Quartet No. 3 E♭ minor
...876), op. 30, CW 92
...N M-2002-0203-8
● 197

...iano Trio A minor
...881-82), op. 50, CW 93
...N 3-7957-6829-2   ISMN M-2002-0233-5
● 251

Telemann, Georg Philipp
(1681-1767)

Choral and Vocal Works

Wider die falschen Propheten
(Beware of False Prophets)
Cantata (Bergmann)
ISMN M-2002-0914-3
ETP 1072

Orchestral Works

Overture (Suite) A minor
for recorder (flute), strings and
basso continuo   (Beechey)
study score
ISBN 3-7957-6863-2   ISMN M-2002-0756-9
ETP 882

solo recorder (flute)
ISMN M-2002-2008-7
EOS 882-21

set of string parts
ISMN M-2002-2010-0
EOS 882-70

separate parts:
violin I
ISMN M-2002-2014-8
EOS 882-11
violin II
ISMN M-2002-2015-5
EOS 882-12
viola
ISMN M-2002-2016-2
EOS 882-13
bassi
ISMN M-2002-2017-9
EOS 882-14
basso continuo
ISBN 3-7957-6906-X   ISMN M-2002-2009-4
EOS 882-65

La Lyra
Overture (Suite) E♭ major   (Bergmann)
study score
ISMN M-2002-1055-2
ETP 1317

separate parts:
violin I
ISMN M-2002-1576-2
PC 76-11
violin II
ISMN M-2002-1577-9
PC 76-12
viola
ISMN M-2002-1578-6
PC 76-13
cello/double bass
ISMN M-2002-1579-3
PC 76-14
harpsichord
ISMN M-2002-1580-9
PC 76-15

Musique de table
3me Production (1733)   (Bergmann)
study score
ISMN M-2002-0755-2
ETP 879

Suite
separate parts:
oboe I
ISMN M-2002-1348-5
PC 37-11
oboe II
ISMN M-2002-1349-2
PC 37-12
violin I
ISMN M-2002-1350-8
PC 37-13
violin II
ISMN M-2002-1351-5
PC 37-14
viola
ISMN M-2002-1352-2
PC 37-15
cello
ISMN M-2002-1353-9
PC 37-16
double bass
ISMN M-2002-1354-6
PC 37-17
harpsichord
ISMN M-2002-1355-3
PC 37-18

Concerto
separate parts:
horn I
ISMN M-2002-1356-0
PC 38-11
horn II
ISMN M-2002-1357-7
PC 38-12
violin I
ISMN M-2002-1358-4
PC 38-13
violin II
ISMN M-2002-1359-1
PC 38-14
viola
ISMN M-2002-1360-7
PC 38-15
cello/double bass
ISMN M-2002-1361-4
PC 38-16
harpsichord
ISMN M-2002-1362-1
PC 38-17

Concertos

Concerto F minor
for oboe, strings and basso continuo
(Schroeder)
study score
ISBN 3-7957-6171-9   ISMN M-2002-0976-1
ETP 1214

solo oboe
ISMN M-2002-1418-5
PC 51-01

separate parts:

violin I
ISMN M-2002-1419-2
PC 51-11

violin II
ISMN M-2002-1420-8
PC 51-12

viola
ISMN M-2002-1421-5
PC 51-13

cello/double bass
ISMN M-2002-1422-2
PC 51-14

harpsichord
ISMN M-2002-1423-9
PC 51-15

Concerto A major
for oboe d'amore, strings and
basso continuo (Schroeder)

study score
ISMN M-2002-0996-9
ETP 1241

solo parts:

oboe d'amore
ISMN M-2002-1569-4
PC 75-01

oboe
ISMN M-2002-1570-0
PC 75-02

separate parts:

violin I
ISMN M-2002-1571-7
PC 75-11

violin II
ISMN M-2002-1572-4
PC 75-12

viola
ISMN M-2002-1573-1
PC 75-13

cello/double bass
ISMN M-2002-1574-8
PC 75-14

harpsichord
ISMN M-2002-1575-5
PC 75-15

Concerto G major
for violin and string orchestra (Schroeder)

study score
ISMN M-2002-0997-6
ETP 1242

solo violin
ISMN M-2002-1563-2
PC 74-01

separate parts:

violin I
ISMN M-2002-1564-9
PC 74-11

violin II
ISMN M-2002-1565-6
PC 74-12

viola
ISMN M-2002-1566-3
PC 74-13

cello/double bass
ISMN M-2002-1567-0
PC 74-14

harpsichord
ISMN M-2002-1568-7
PC 74-15

Concerto à 6 in E minor
for flute and orchestra
(Schroeder)

study score
ISMN M-2002-0999-0
ETP 1244

solo flute
ISMN M-2002-1581-6
PC 77-01

separate parts:

violin I
ISMN M-2002-1582-3
PC 77-11

violin II
ISMN M-2002-1583-0
PC 77-12

viola I
ISMN M-2002-1584-7
PC 77-13

viola II
ISMN M-2002-1585-4
PC 77-14

cello/double bass
ISMN M-2002-1586-1
PC 77-15

harpsichord
ISMN M-2002-1587-8
PC 77-16

Concerto D major
for flute and string orchestra (Schroeder)

study score
ISBN 3-7957-6295-2   ISMN M-2002-1022-4
ETP 1268

solo flute
ISMN M-2002-1741-4
PC 107-01

separate parts:

violin I
ISMN M-2002-1742-1
PC 107-11

violin II
ISMN M-2002-1743-8
PC 107-12

viola
ISMN M-2002-1744-5
PC 107-13

bassi
ISMN M-2002-1745-2
PC 107-14

harpsichord
ISMN M-2002-1746-9
PC 107-15

Concerto E minor
for 2 flutes, violin, strings and
basso continuo (Schroeder)

study score
ISMN M-2002-0986-0
ETP 1226

solo violin
ISMN M-2002-1469-7
PC 60-01

separate parts:

flute I
ISMN M-2002-1470-3
PC 60-11

flute II
ISMN M-2002-1471-0
PC 60-12

violin I
ISMN M-2002-1472-7
PC 60-13

violin II
ISMN M-2002-1473-4
PC 60-14

viola
ISMN M-2002-1474-1
PC 60-15

double bass
ISMN M-2002-1475-8
PC 60-16

harpsichord
ISMN M-2002-1476-5
PC 60-17

Tippett, Michael
(1905-1998)

Concerto for Double String Orchestra
(1938-39)
ISMN M-2002-1063-7
ETP 1331   (L)

Fantasia Concertante on a Theme of Corelli
for string orchestra (1953) (Kemp)
ISBN 3-7957-6844-6   ISMN M-2002-1116-0
ETP 1395   (L)

Little Music
for string orchestra (1946)
ISMN M-2002-1064-4
ETP 1332   (L)

Suite in D
for the Birthday of Prince Charles (1948)
ISMN M-2002-1072-9
ETP 1342   (L)

Touchemoulin, Joseph
(1727-1801)

ncerto A major
flute and strings (Braun)
dy score
ɅN M-2002-1030-9
ꓑ 1276

lo flute
ɅN M-2002-1770-4
112-01

parate parts:
lin I
ɅN M-2002-1771-1
112-11

lin II
ɅN M-2002-1772-8
112-12

la
ɅN M-2002-1773-5
112-13

ssi
ɅN M-2002-1774-2
112-14

Vaughan Williams, Ralph
(1872-1958)

ymphonies
ennedy)
. 4 F minor
BN 3-7957-7118-8   ISMN M-2002-1131-3
P 1505

. 5 D major
BN 3-7957-6870-5   ISMN M-2002-1132-0
P 1506

. 6 E minor
BN 3-7957-6731-8   ISMN M-2002-1133-7
P 1507

e Lark Ascending
mance for violin and orchestra (Kennedy)
BN 3-7957-6924-8   ISMN M-2002-1109-2
P 1388

oncerto F minor
bass tuba and orchestra (Kennedy)
BN 3-7957-6794-6   ISMN M-2002-1155-9
P 1811

Verdi, Guiseppe
(1813-1901)

horal and Vocal Works

uattro Pezzi Sacri
BN 3-7957-6955-8   ISMN M-2002-0844-3
P 1000

Messa da Requiem
ISBN 3-7957-6918-3   ISMN M-2002-0822-1
ETP 975

Overtures

La Forza del Destino
(The Force of Destiny /
Die Macht des Schicksals)
ISBN 3-7957-6124-7   ISMN M-2002-0942-6
ETP 1107

Nabucco
ISBN 3-7957-6162-X   ISMN M-2002-0947-1
ETP 1112

I vespri siciliani
(Sicilian Vespers / Die sizilianische Vesper)
ISBN 3-7957-6140-9   ISMN M-2002-0943-3
ETP 1108

Chamber Music

String Quartet E minor
ISBN 3-7957-6273-1   ISMN M-2002-0206-9
ETP 207

Victoria, Tomás Luis de
(1755-1824)

Motet and Mass
„O quam gloriosum est regnum" (Rive)
ISMN M-2002-1144-3
ETP 1706

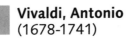

Viotti, Giovanni Battista
(1755-1824)

Concerto No. 22 A minor
for violin and orchestra (Einstein)
ISMN M-2002-0657-9
ETP 756

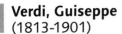

Vivaldi, Antonio
(1678-1741)

Choral and Vocal Works

Kyrie
RV 587 (Braun)
ISMN M-2002-0928-0
ETP 1090

Lauda Jerusalem
Psalm 147, RV 609 (Braun)
ISMN M-2002-0923-5
ETP 1081

Concertos

L'Estro Armonico, op. 3
study score
Nos. 1-12 complete in 1 volume (Hogwood)
ISBN 3-7957-6964-7   ISMN M-2002-2051-3
ETP 1871-82

No. 1 D major, RV 549 / PV 146
for 4 violins, strings and b.c.
study score
ISBN 3-7957-6219-7   ISMN M-2002-1012-5
ETP 1258

separate parts:
violin I
ISMN M-2002-1659-2
PC 92-12

violin II
ISMN M-2002-1660-8
PC 92-13

violine III
ISMN M-2002-1661-5
PC 92-14

violine IV
ISMN M-2002-1662-2
PC 92-15

viola I
ISMN M-2002-1663-9
PC 92-16

viola II
ISMN M-2002-1664-6
PC 92-17

bassi
ISMN M-2002-1665-3
PC 92-18

harpsichord
ISMN M-2002-1658-5
PC 92-11

set of string parts (Hogwood)
ISMN M-2002-2160-2
EOS 1871-70   i.V. / in prep.

No. 2 G minor, RV 578 / PV 326
for 2 violins, cello obligato and strings
study score
ISMN M-2002-0673-9
ETP 772

No. 6 A minor, RV 356 / PV 1
for violin, strings and b.c.
study score
(Einstein)
ISBN 3-7957-6876-4   ISMN M-2002-0654-8
ETP 753

set of string parts
(Hogwood)
ISMN M-2002-2204-3
EOS 1876-70   i.V. / in prep.
separate parts   i.V. / in prep.

No. 7 F major, RV 567 / PV 249
for 4 violins, cello and strings (Eller)
study score
ISBN 3-7957-7108-0   ISMN M-2002-1032-3
ETP 1278

separate parts:
violin I
ISMN M-2002-1782-7
PC 114-11

violin II
ISMN M-2002-1783-4
PC 114-12

violine III
ISMN M-2002-1784-1
PC 114-13

violine IV
ISMN M-2002-1785-8
PC 114-14

viola I
ISMN M-2002-1786-5
PC 114-15

viola II
ISMN M-2002-1787-2
PC 114-16

cello
ISMN M-2002-1788-9
PC 114-17

double bass
ISMN M-2002-1789-6
PC 114-18

harpsichord
ISMN M-2002-1790-2
PC 114-19

set of string parts
(Hogwood)
ISMN M-2002-2212-8
EOS 1877-70   i.V. / in prep.
separate parts   i.V. / in prep.

No. 8 A minor, RV 522
for 2 violins, strings and basso continuo
study score
(Einstein)
ISBN 3-7957-6626-5   ISMN M-2002-0663-0
ETP 762
set of string parts
(Hogwood)
ISMN M-2002-2221-0
EOS 1878-70   i.V. / in prep.
separate parts   i.V. / in prep.

No. 9 D major, RV 230 / PV 147
for violin
study score
(Eller)
ISBN 3-7957-6182-4   ISMN M-2002-1014-9
ETP 1260
set of string parts
(Hogwood)
ISMN M-2002-2230-2
EOS 1879-70   i.V. / in prep.
separate parts   i.V. / in prep.

No. 10 B minor, RV 580 / PV 97
for 4 violins, strings and basso continuo
study score
(Einstein)
ISBN 3-7957-6901-9   ISMN M-2002-0650-0
ETP 749

set of string parts
(Hogwood)
ISMN M-2002-2238-8
EOS 1880-70   i.V. / in prep.
separate parts   i.V. / in prep.

No. 11 D minor, RV 565 / PV 250
for 2 violins, strings and basso continuo
study score
(Einstein)
ISBN 3-7957-6689-3   ISMN M-2002-0651-7
ETP 750
set of string parts
(Hogwood)
ISMN M-2002-2247-0
EOS 1881-70   i.V. / in prep.
separate parts   i.V. / in prep.

Concerto G minor, op. 6/1
for violin, strings and b.c. , RV 324 / PV 329
(Einstein)
study score
ISMN M-2002-0655-5
ETP 754
separate parts:
violin I solo/rip.
ISMN M-2002-1214-3
PC 6-11

violin II
ISMN M-2002-1215-0
PC 6-12

viola
ISMN M-2002-1216-7
PC 6-13

cello/double bass
ISMN M-2002-1217-4
PC 6-14

harpsichord
ISMN M-2002-1218-1
PC 6-15

Concerto D major, op. 7/11
„Grosso Mogul", RV 208 / PV 151
for violin, strings and b.c. (Schroeder)
study score
ISMN M-2002-0994-5
ETP 1237
solo violin
ISMN M-2002-1553-3
PC 72-01
separate parts:
violin I
ISMN M-2002-1554-0
PC 72-11

violin II
ISMN M-2002-1555-7
PC 72-12

viola
ISMN M-2002-1556-4
PC 72-13

bassi
ISMN M-2002-1557-1
PC 72-14

harpsichord
ISMN M-2002-1558-8
PC 72-15

Concerto D major, op. 7/12
for violin, strings and b.c. , RV 214 / PV 152
(Schroeder)
study score
ISMN M-2002-0987-7
ETP 1227
solo violin
ISMN M-2002-1497-0
PC 63-01
separate parts:
violin I
ISMN M-2002-1498-7
PC 63-11

violin II
ISMN M-2002-1499-4
PC 63-12

viola
ISMN M-2002-1500-7
PC 63-13

double bass/cello
ISMN M-2002-1501-4
PC 63-14

harpsichord
ISMN M-2002-1502-1
PC 63-15

La Quattro Stagione, op. 8
(The Four Seasons / Die vier Jahreszeiten)
Concertos for violin, strings and b. c.
study score
complete in 1 volume (Launchbury)
ISBN 3-7957-6676-1   ISMN M-2002-0982-2
ETP 1220-23

No. 1 E major "Primavera"
("Spring" / "Der Frühling")
RV 269 / PV 241
study score
ISBN 3-7957-6637-0   ISMN M-2002-0981-5
ETP 1220
solo violin
ISMN M-2002-1851-0
EOS 1220-01
set of string parts
ISMN M-2002-1857-2
EOS 1220-70
separate parts:
violin I
ISMN M-2002-1852-7
EOS 1220-11

violin II
ISMN M-2002-1853-4
EOS 1220-12

viola
ISMN M-2002-1854-1
EOS 1220-13

cello
ISMN M-2002-1855-8
EOS 1220-14

basso continuo
ISMN M-2002-1856-5
EOS 1220-65

. 2 G minor "L'Estate"
ummer" / "Der Sommer")
315 / PV 336

udy score
3N 3-7957-6670-2   ISMN M-2002-0983-9
P 1221

lo violin
MN M-2002-1858-9
S 1221-01

t of string parts
MN M-2002-1864-0
S 1221-70

parate parts:
lin I
MN M-2002-1859-6
S 1221-11

lin II
MN M-2002-1860-2
S 1221-12

la
MN M-2002-1861-9
S 1221-13

llo
MN M-2002-1862-6
S 1221-14

sso continuo
MN M-2002-1863-3
S 1221-65

. 3 F major "L'Autunno"
Autumn" / "Der Herbst")
293 / PV 257

udy score
BN 3-7957-6671-0   ISMN M-2002-0984-6
P 1222

lo violin
MN M-2002-1865-7
S 1222-01

t of string parts
MN M-2002-1871-8
S 1222-70

parate parts:
olin I
MN M-2002-1866-4
S 1222-11

olin II
MN M-2002-1867-1
S 1222-12

la
MN M-2002-1868-8
S 1222-13

llo
MN M-2002-1869-5
S 1222-14

asso continuo
MN M-2002-1870-1
S 1222-65

. 4 F minor "L'Inverno"
Winter" / "Der Winter")
297 / PV 442

tudy score
BN 3-7957-6638-9   ISMN M-2002-0985-3
P 1223

solo violin
ISMN M-2002-1872-5
EOS 1223-01

set of string parts
ISMN M-2002-1878-7
EOS 1223-70

separate parts:
violin I
ISMN M-2002-1873-2
EOS 1223-11

violin II
ISMN M-2002-1874-9
EOS 1223-12

viola
ISMN M-2002-1875-6
EOS 1223-13

cello
ISMN M-2002-1876-3
EOS 1223-14

basso continuo
ISMN M-2002-1877-0
EOS 1223-65

Concerti grossi "La Cetra"
("The Zither")
for violin, strings and b. c., op. 9 (Schroeder)

No. 10 G major, RV 300 / PV 103
study score
ISBN 3-7957-6795-4   ISMN M-2002-1001-9
ETP 1246

solo violin
ISMN M-2002-1601-1
PC 81-01

separate parts:
violin I
ISMN M-2002-1602-8
PC 81-11

violin II
ISMN M-2002-1603-5
PC 81-12

viola
ISMN M-2002-1604-2
PC 81-13

cello/double bass
ISMN M-2002-1605-9
PC 81-14

harpsichord
ISMN M-2002-1606-6
PC 81-15

No. 11 C minor, RV 198
study score
ISBN 3-7957-6344-4   ISMN M-2002-1003-3
ETP 1248

solo violin
ISMN M-2002-1607-3
PC 82-01

separate parts:
violin I
ISMN M-2002-1608-0
PC 82-11

violin II
ISMN M-2002-1609-7
PC 82-12

viola
ISMN M-2002-1610-3
PC 82-13

cello
ISMN M-2002-1611-0
PC 82-14

harpsichord
ISMN M-2002-1612-7
PC 82-15

Concerto D major, op. 10/3
"Il Gardellino"
("The Gold-finch" / "Der Distelfink")
for flute, strings and b.c., RV 428 / PV 155
(Einstein)

study score
ISMN M-2002-0659-3
ETP 758

solo flute
ISMN M-2002-1333-1
PC 31-01

separate parts:
violin I
ISMN M-2002-1334-8
PC 31-11

violin II
ISMN M-2002-1335-5
PC 31-12

viola
ISMN M-2002-1336-2
PC 31-13

cello/double bass
ISMN M-2002-1337-9
PC 31-14

harpsichord
ISMN M-2002-1338-6
PC 31-15

Concerto D minor, op. 26/9
for cello, strings and b.c., RV 406/481
(Schroeder)

study score
ISMN M-2002-1005-7
ETP 1250

solo cello
ISMN M-2002-1619-6
PC 84-01

separate parts:
violin I
ISMN M-2002-1621-9
PC 84-12

violin II
ISMN M-2002-1622-6
PC 84-13

viola
ISMN M-2002-1623-3
PC 84-14

cello/double bass
ISMN M-2002-1624-0
PC 84-15

harpsichord
ISMN M-2002-1620-2
PC 84-11

Concerto D major, op. 35/19
fatto per la Solennita della Lingua di
San Antonio (Jenkins)
for violin, strings and b.c. , RV 212a / PV 165
study score
ISMN M-2002-0979-2
ETP 1217
solo violin
ISMN M-2002-1429-1
PC 53-01
separate parts:
violin I/II
ISMN M-2002-1430-7
PC 53-11
viola
ISMN M-2002-1431-4
PC 53-12
cello/double bass
ISMN M-2002-1432-1
PC 53-13
harpsichord
ISMN M-2002-1433-8
PC 53-14

Concerti, op. 44
(Schroeder)
No. 11 C major, RV 443 / PV 79
for flautino (recorder), strings and b.c.
study score
ISBN 3-7957-6186-7   ISMN M-2002-1002-6
ETP 1247
solo flautino (recorder)
ISMN M-2002-1613-4
PC 83-01
separate parts:
violin I
ISMN M-2002-1614-1
PC 83-11
violin II
ISMN M-2002-1615-8
PC 83-12
viola
ISMN M-2002-1616-5
PC 83-13
cello/double bass
ISMN M-2002-1617-2
PC 83-14
harpsichord/piano
ISMN M-2002-1618-9
PC 83-15

No. 16 F major, RV 98 / PV 261
„La tempesta di mare"
for flute, oboe, bassoon, strings and b.c.
study score
ISMN M-2002-1010-1
ETP 1256
solo parts:
flute
ISMN M-2002-1666-0
PC 93-01
oboe
ISMN M-2002-1667-7
PC 93-02

bassoon
ISMN M-2002-1668-4
PC 93-03
separate parts:
violin I
ISMN M-2002-1669-1
PC 93-11
violin II
ISMN M-2002-1670-7
PC 93-12
viola
ISMN M-2002-1671-4
PC 93-13
cello/double bass
ISMN M-2002-1672-1
PC 93-14
harpsichord
ISMN M-2002-1673-8
PC 93-15

No. 19 C minor, RV 441 / PV 440
for flute (treble recorder), strings and b.c.
study score
ISMN M-2002-1033-0
ETP 1280
solo flute (recorder)
ISMN M-2002-1791-9
PC 117-01
separate parts:
violin I
ISMN M-2002-1792-6
PC 117-11
violin II
ISMN M-2002-1793-3
PC 117-12
viola
ISMN M-2002-1794-0
PC 117-13
cello/double bass
ISMN M-2002-1795-7
PC 117-14
harpsichord
ISMN M-2002-1796-4
PC 117-15

Concerto B♭ major, op. 45/8
„La Notte", RV 501 / PV 401
for bassoon, strings and b.c. (Schroeder)
study score
ISMN M-2002-1008-8
ETP 1254
solo bassoon
ISMN M-2002-1632-5
PC 86-01
separate parts:
violin I
ISMN M-2002-1633-2
PC 86-11
violin II
ISMN M-2002-1634-9
PC 86-12
viola
ISMN M-2002-1635-6
PC 86-13

cello/double bass
ISMN M-2002-1636-3
PC 86-14
harpsichord
ISMN M-2002-1637-0
PC 86-15

Concerto C major, op. 46/1
for 2 trumpets, strings and basso continuo,
RV 537 / PV 75 (Schroeder)
study score
ISBN 3-7957-6153-0   ISMN M-2002-1011-8
ETP 1257
solo parts:
trumpet I
ISMN M-2002-1651-6
PC 91-01
trumpet II
ISMN M-2002-1652-3
PC 91-02
separate parts:
violin I
ISMN M-2002-1654-7
PC 91-12
violin II
ISMN M-2002-1655-4
PC 91-13
viola
ISMN M-2002-1656-1
PC 91-14
cello/double bass/bassoon
ISMN M-2002-1657-8
PC 91-15
harpsichord
ISMN M-2002-1653-0
PC 91-11

Concerto F major, op. 46/2
for 2 french horns, 2 oboes, bassoon,
violin, strings and b.c., RV 569 / PV 273
study score
ISMN M-2002-1031-6
ETP 1277
solo violin
ISMN M-2002-1775-9
PC 113-01
wind band parts
ISMN M-2002-1776-6
PC 113-10
separate parts:
violin I
ISMN M-2002-1777-3
PC 113-11
violin II
ISMN M-2002-1778-0
PC 113-12
viola
ISMN M-2002-1779-7
PC 113-13
cello/double bass
ISMN M-2002-1780-3
PC 113-14
organ/harpsichord
ISMN M-2002-1781-0
PC 113-15

ncerto grosso C major
2 flutes, strings and b.c., op. 47/2
533 / PV 76 (Schroeder)
ıdy score
ıN M-2002-1006-4
P 1252
lo parts:
te I
ıN M-2002-1625-7
85-01
te II
ıN M-2002-1626-4
85-02
parate parts:
lin I
ıN M-2002-1628-8
85-12
lin II
ıN M-2002-1629-5
85-13
la
ıN M-2002-1630-1
85-14
lo/double bass/bassoon
ıN M-2002-1631-8
85-15
rpsichord
ıN M-2002-1627-1
85-11

ncerto G major, op. 51/4
lla Rustica", RV 151 / PV 143
string orchestra and basso continuo
:hroeder)
ıdy score
BN 3-7957-6865-9   ISMN M-2002-1009-5
P 1255
eparate parts:
lin I
ıN M-2002-1639-4
87-12
lin II
ıN M-2002-1640-0
87-13
la
ıN M-2002-1641-7
87-14
llo/double bass
ıN M-2002-1642-4
87-15
rpsichord
ıN M-2002-1638-7
87-11

ncerto F major, op. 64/4
violin, organ, strings and basso continuo,
542 / PV 274 (Schroeder)
ıdy score
BN 3-7957-6292-8   ISMN M-2002-1027-9
P 1273
lo parts:
lin
ıN M-2002-1747-6
108-01

---

organ
ISMN M-2002-1748-3
PC 108-02
separate parts:
violin I
ISMN M-2002-1749-0
PC 108-11
violin II
ISMN M-2002-1750-6
PC 108-12
viola
ISMN M-2002-1751-3
PC 108-13
cello/bassoon/double bass
ISMN M-2002-1752-0
PC 108-14
harpsichord
ISMN M-2002-1753-7
PC 108-15

Wagner, Richard
(1813-1883)

Operas
Der Ring des Nibelungen
Das Rheingold, WWV 86 A
(from the new Complete Edition) (Voss)
ISBN 3-7957-6296-0   ISMN M-2002-2052-0
ETP 8059

Die Walküre, WWV 86 B
ISBN 3-7957-6279-0   ISMN M-2002-0774-3
ETP 908

Siegfried, WWV 86 C
ISBN 3-7957-6275-8   ISMN M-2002-0775-0
ETP 909

Götterdämmerung, WWV 86D
(from the new Complete Edition) (Fladt)
ISBN 3-7957-6309-6   ISMN M-2002-2054-4
ETP 8057

Der fliegende Holländer
(The Flying Duchtman), WWV 63
ISBN 3-7957-6216-2   ISMN M-2002-0768-2
ETP 902

Lohengrin, WWV 75
(including variants of the Paris arrangement)
ISBN 3-7957-6215-4   ISMN M-2002-0770-5
ETP 904

Die Meistersinger von Nürnberg, WWV 96
(The Mastersingers of Nuremberg) (Voss)
(from the new Complete Edition)
ISBN 3-7957-6179-4   ISMN M-2002-1987-6
ETP 8033

Parsifal, WWV 111
(from the new Complete Edition)
ISBN 3-7957-6337-1   ISMN M-2002-2311-8
ETP 8058

Tannhäuser und der Sängerkrieg auf Wartburg
(including variants of the Paris arrangement)
WWV 70
ISMN M-2002-0769-9
ETP 903

Tristan und Isolde, WWV 90
scenario in three acts (Vetter/Voss)
(from the new Complete Edition)
ISBN 3-7957-6210-3   ISMN M-2002-2004-9
ETP 8052

Orchestral Works
Overtures and Preludes
Eine Faust-Ouvertüre, WWV 59
ISMN M-2002-0583-1
ETP 671

Der fliegende Holländer, WWV 63
(The Flying Dutchman)
ISBN 3-7957-6882-9   ISMN M-2002-0581-7
ETP 668   (L)

Lohengrin, WWV 75
Preludes to Acts 1 and 3
ISMN M-2002-0566-4
ETP 652

Die Meistersinger von Nürnberg
ISBN 3-7957-6930-2   ISMN M-2002-0578-7
ETP 665

Die Meistersinger von Nürnberg
Introduction to Act 3
ISMN M-2002-0721-7
ETP 825

Parsifal, WWV 111
ISMN M-2002-0579-4
ETP 666

Rienzi, WWV 49
ISBN 3-7957-6807-1   ISMN M-2002-0580-0
ETP 667   (L)

Tannhäuser, WWV 70
Overture
ISBN 3-7957-6927-2   ISMN M-2002-0582-4
ETP 669   (L)

Introduction to Act 3 (Tannhäuser's Pilgrimage)
ISMN M-2002-0714-9
ETP 815

Tristan und Isolde
Prelude and Liebestod, WWV 90
ISBN 3-7957-6663-X   ISMN M-2002-0563-3
ETP 649

Die Walküre, WWV 86 B
Der Ritt der Walküren (Orchesterstück)
(The Ride of the Valkyries)
ISMN M-2002-0707-1
ETP 807   (L)

Wotans Abschied und Feuerzauber
(Wotan's Farewell and Magic Fire Music)
for bass and orchestra
ISMN M-2002-0708-8
ETP 808   (L)

Siegfried-Idyll, WWV 103
ISBN 3-7957-7104-8   ISMN M-2002-0710-1
ETP 810

Götterdämmerung, WWV 86 D
Trauermusik (Funeral Music)
ISMN M-2002-0711-8
ETP 811

Parsifal, WWV 111
Karfreitagszauber (Good Friday Music)
ISMN M-2002-0712-5
ETP 812   (L)

Tannhäuser, WWV 70
Bacchanale (Orchesterstück)
ISMN M-2002-0713-2
ETP 814

Wesendonck-Lieder, WWV 91
for soprano and orchestra (Salter)
ISBN 3-7957-6894-2   ISMN M-2002-1145-0
ETP 1707

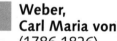

Weber, Carl Maria von (1786-1826)

Opera

Der Freischütz
op. 77, JV 277 (Abert/Haan)
ISMN M-2002-0781-1
ETP 915

Orchestral Works

Symphony No. 1 C major
(1807/10), JV 50 (Oeser)
ISBN 3-7957-6154-9   ISMN M-2002-0511-4
ETP 591   (L)

Symphony No. 2 C major
(1807), JV 51 (Schönzeler)
ISMN M-2002-0512-1
ETP 592   (L)

Aufforderung zum Tanz
(Invitation to the Dance), op. 65, JV 260
ISMN M-2002-0726-2
ETP 831

Overtures

Abu Hassan, J 160 / WeV C. 6
ISMN M-2002-0600-5
ETP 696

Der Beherrscher der Geister
(The Ruler of the Spirits), op. 27, J 122
Recast of the lost Overture to the unfinished
Opera "Rübezahl"
ISMN M-2002-0525-1
ETP 605

Euryanthe, op. 81, JV 291
ISBN 3-7957-6761-X   ISMN M-2002-0554-1
ETP 635   (L)

Der Freischütz, op. 77, JV 277
ISBN 3-7957-6678-8   ISMN M-2002-0522-0
ETP 602

Jubilee Overture, op. 59, J 245
ISMN M-2002-0532-9
ETP 612   (L)

Oberon, JV 306
ISBN 3-7957-6926-4   ISMN M-2002-0527-5
ETP 607

Peter Schmoll, op. 8, JV 8
ISBN 3-7957-6979-5   ISMN M-2002-0946-4
ETP 1111

Preciosa, op. 78, J 279/WeV F. 22
ISMN M-2002-0529-9
ETP 609   (L)

Silvana, J 87
ISMN M-2002-0601-2
ETP 697

Concertos

Piano Concerto No. 2 E♭ major
op. 32, JV 155
ISMN M-2002-0990-7
ETP 1230   (L)

Konzertstück F minor
for piano and orchestra, op. 79
ISBN 3-7957-6959-0   ISMN M-2002-0647-0
ETP 746   (L)

Cello Concerto (Fantasie)
Grand Potpourri, op. 20, J 64 (Beyer)
ISMN M-2002-1035-4
ETP 1282   (L)

Clarinet Concerto No. 1 F minor
op. 73, JV 114
ISBN 3-7957-6734-2   ISMN M-2002-0694-4
ETP 793   (L)

Clarinet Concerto No. 2 E♭ major
op. 74, JV 118
ISBN 3-7957-6773-3   ISMN M-2002-0695-1
ETP 794

Clarinet Concertino E♭ major
op. 26, JV 109
ISBN 3-7957-6711-3   ISMN M-2002-0970-9
ETP 1205

Bassoon Concerto F major
op. 75, JV 127
ISBN 3-7957-6326-6   ISMN M-2002-0966-2
ETP 1201

Chamber Music

Quintet B♭ major, op. 34
for clarinet and string quartet, JV 182;
ISBN 3-7957-6159-X   ISMN M-2002-0322-6
ETP 384

Trio G minor, op. 63
for flute (or violin), cello and piano, J 259
ISMN M-2002-0337-0
ETP 400

Werner, Gregorius Joseph (1695-1766)

Weihnachtslied
„Wir seynd geg'n euch wahrhafte Freund"
Kantate (1757) (Falvy)
study score (= choral score)
ISMN M-2002-0926-6
ETP 1084

separate parts:
violin I
ISMN M-2002-1802-2
PC 120-11
violin II
ISMN M-2002-1803-9
PC 120-12
viola
ISMN M-2002-1804-6
PC 120-13
cello/double bass
ISMN M-2002-1805-3
PC 120-14
organ
ISMN M-2002-1806-0
PC 120-15

Wolf, Hugo (1860-1903)

Italian Serenade G major
version for small orchestra
ISBN 3-7957-7148-X   ISMN M-2002-1059-0
ETP 1322

String Quartet D minor
Entbehren sollst du, sollst entbehren
ISMN M-2002-0260-1
ETP 285

Italian Serenade G major
for string quartet
ISBN 3-7957-6909-4   ISMN M-2002-0261-8
ETP 286

Wolf-Ferrari, Ermanno (1876-1948)

Il Segreto di Susanns
(Susanna's Secret / Susannens Geheimnis)
Overture
ISMN M-2002-0956-3
ETP 1125